YOUNG STUDENTS

Learning Library®

VOLUME 12

Knighthood — Malta

WEEKLY READER BOOKS

MIDDLETOWN · CONNECTICUT

PHOTO CREDITS

Contents

KNIGHTHOOD

KNIGHTHOOD In early medieval times in Europe, military battles were fought between soldiers on horseback. These mounted warriors fought each other with swords and lances. They carried shields and wore armor to protect themselves. These warriors were called *knights* in English, *chevaliers* in French, *Ritters* in German, and *caballeros* in Spanish. The French chevalier Bayard, who lived from about 1474 to 1524, was one of the most famous knights of all time. Known as "the brave and virtuous knight," he was fearless in battle and generous to all persons.

In the early days, knights were landowners who owed allegiance (pledged loyalty) to a lord—a king, a prince, or a nobleman. The lord protected the landowner from bandits and robbers. In return, the landowner agreed to fight against his lord's enemies. This arrangement was part of the organization of society known as the feudal system.

The landowners could not stay away at war for a very long time, since they had to look after their lands and families. But a nobleman fighting a long war needed soldiers he could depend upon. Gradually the custom developed that a landowner's youngest son would serve in his father's place in the nobleman's army.

A young man first had to prove that he knew how to ride a horse and use a sword. Contests were held in which young men fought against each other in a mock battle. These contests were called *tournaments*, or *tourneys*. If a young man proved he was a good fighter, he was knighted by the nobleman. In this ceremony, the young man would kneel before the nobleman. The nobleman would touch him on the shoulder with a sword and say,

"I dub thee Sir John" or whatever the young man's first name was. "Sir" was the English title of knighthood.

After a great many years, a complicated system developed for training young men to be knights. A young boy of seven or eight would leave his family. He would become a *page* at a nobleman's castle. He waited on tables, ran errands, and was brought up in the castle as if he were a distant relative of the nobleman. He also began to learn the things a knight had to know to be a good and brave warrior.

When the boy was a teenager, he became a *squire*, or servant, to a knight. The knight taught him how to ride a horse and how to fight with weapons. The squire took part in tournaments. Whenever the knight rode through the countryside, the squire rode with him and carried the knight's sword and armor. The squire helped the knight put on his armor before a battle. He followed the knight into battle carrying his banner. If the squire proved himself brave and faithful, he was knighted at a special ceremony. He spent the whole night before the ceremony in prayer before the altar of a church. This was called a *vigil*. In the morning, he was dressed in a white robe and knightly armor. His lord then dubbed him knight.

▲ *To train for battle, and to show off their skills, knights took part in mock fights. These were known as jousts. Such contests took place in front of an audience at open-air tournaments, or* tourneys.

When gunpowder first appeared on the battlefield, knights did not immediately stop wearing armor. They had thicker armor made, which became so heavy that if they fell off their horses, they lay where they landed, unable to get up.

◄ *Lasers are used extensively in drilling operations where great accuracy is required. Here a hole is being drilled in aluminum. (See* LASERS AND MASERS.*)*

KNITTING

In the 1100's, knights took part in tournaments that lasted all day and involved large numbers of fighters. These tournaments often led to violence all around the district in which they took place. The English government tried to stop these tournaments because they could easily lead to rebellion. At that time, the church refused Christian burial to anyone killed in a tournament.

The knights were expected to be more than just warriors. When they were knighted, they swore to obey certain rules of behavior called the code of *chivalry*—although not all knights kept to their oaths. Knights were expected to be courteous and helpful to women. A knight would wear his lady's scarf into battle. The greatest honor for a knight was to be sent on a dangerous *quest*, or mission.

During the holy wars known as the Crusades, religious orders of knights were formed. The knights who joined these orders took an oath of poverty and obedience, as if they were monks. They also swore they would fight to free the Holy Land from the Muslims. The most famous were the Knights Templars and the Knights Hospitalers (later called the Knights of Malta).

When methods of warfare began to change about 500 years ago, the warrior knights were no longer needed. The order of knighthood has now become an honor that is given for outstanding accomplishment.

ALSO READ: ARMOR; ARTHUR, KING; CRUSADES; FEUDALISM; MIDDLE AGES; NOBILITY; WAR.

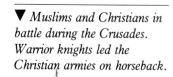

▼ *Muslims and Christians in battle during the Crusades. Warrior knights led the Christian armies on horseback.*

KNITTING Knitting is the art of weaving yarn with needles to form fabric. People first began to knit by hand more than 2,000 years ago. Today, knitting has become a well-developed machine industry.

A hand-knitter usually works with a single length of yarn, looping it with long sticks (*needles*) to form interlocking chains. The knitter can make patterns by using different combinations of two basic stitches, called *knit* and *purl*.

The knitting machine was invented by William Lee of England in 1589. It had hundreds of needles, instead of just two or four. But Queen Elizabeth I would not grant him a patent, and he could not find a rich person to give him money to set up a factory. Only after Lee had died, in 1610, was his brother able to find a rich merchant who was interested. The new machines caused a revolution in the textiles industry, because woolen garments were now much cheaper. Machines today make sweaters, mittens, hats, stockings, and dresses, and knit fabrics that can be cut and sewn like cloth. Hand-knitting has almost disappeared as an industry.

■ LEARN BY DOING

If you are a beginner at knitting, you can start by making a scarf. You will need a pair of size 11 knitting needles and one 4-ounce or 100 g *skein* (coil) of 4-ply wool or synthetic yarn.

First you must *cast on* (put stitches onto one needle). Pull out of the skein yarn equal to three lengths of the needle. Make a loop (a slip knot) as in Diagram 1. Slide the needle into the loop. Pull the loop around the needle (Diagram 2), and tighten the stitch.

To add stitches to the needle, wrap the yarn around your left thumb. Slide the needle in your right hand between your thumb and the yarn around it. Look at Diagram 3. Move the yarn in the right hand over the point of the needle from the back (Diagram 4). Put the loop on your left thumb over the needle point. Look at Diagram 5. Fit the stitch snugly on the needle. Cast on 30 stitches.

To make the scarf, you will knit two rows, then purl two rows, and so on, until the scarf is as long as you want it. To *knit*, place the needle with the stitches on it in your left hand. Insert the right needle through the first stitch on the left needle. Make sure that the right needle is behind the left needle. See Diagram 6. Using the right hand, put the yarn around the back side of the right needle. Look at Diagram 7. Slide the yarn through the loop, as shown in Diagram 8. Remove the stitch from the left needle, as shown in Diagram 9. Knit two rows.

To *purl*, insert the right needle in front of the left needle containing the stitches. Look at Diagram 10. Place the yarn around the right needle from the right side, as shown in Diagram 11. Bring the right needle through the stitch, as shown in Diagram 12. Remove the old stitch from the left needle.

When the scarf is as long as you want it, you must *bind off*. Slip the first stitch from the left needle onto the right needle. Knit the second stitch on the left needle. Put the left needle into the first stitch. Slide the first stitch over the second stitch. Look at Diagram 13. Keep sliding the first stitch so that it comes off the needle. Continue this procedure until one stitch remains on the right needle. Cut the yarn so that a piece four inches (10 cm) long remains. Bring the loose end through the loop and pull tightly. ∎

ALSO READ: NEEDLEWORK.

1 Casting on

2 Casting on

3 Casting on

4 Casting on

5 Casting on

6 Knit

7 Knit

8 Knit

9 Knit

10 Purl

11 Purl

12 Purl

13 Binding off

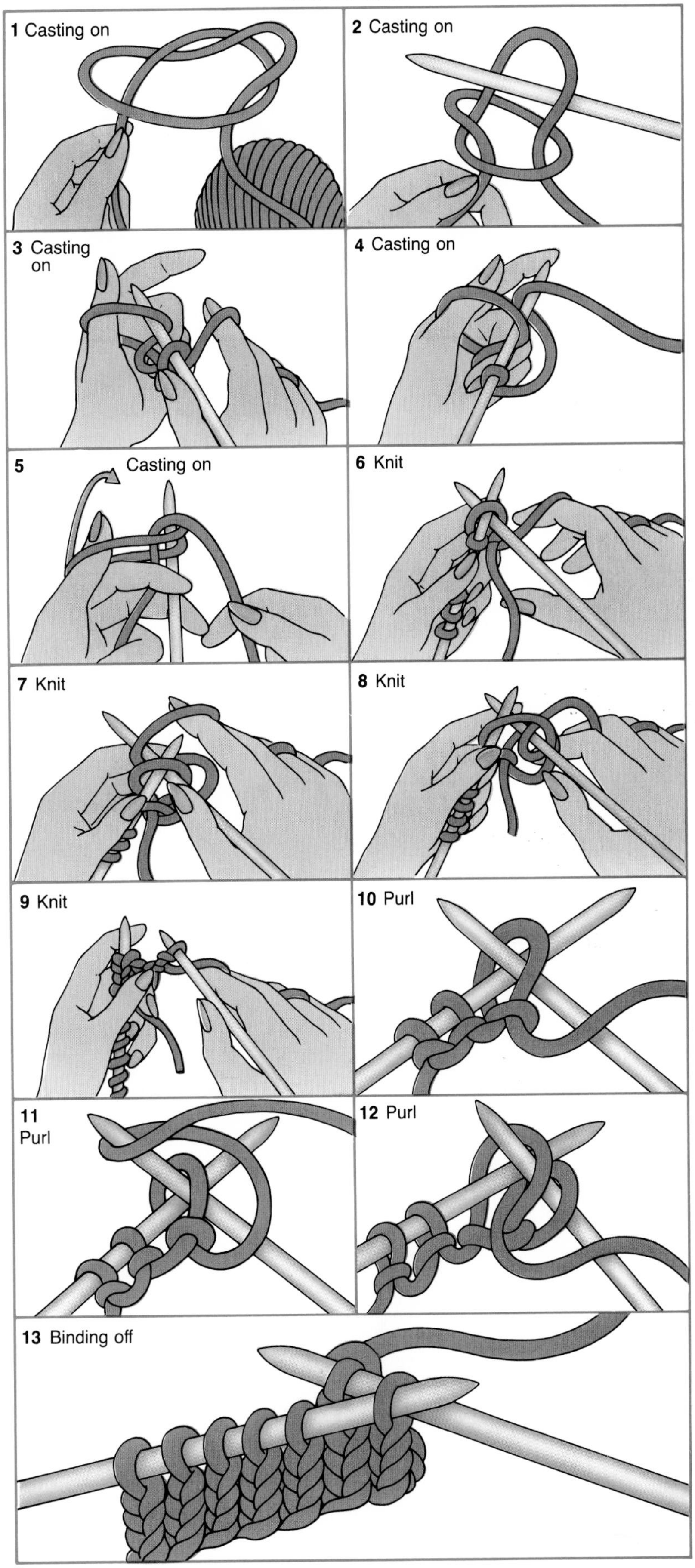

The square knot is the one we all use most. It is easy to tie and untie. But it is not the strongest of knots, especially if the two ropes or cords are of different thicknesses. It has been calculated that the average square knot is only half as strong as an unknotted rope.

KNOT Knots are divided into groups according to how they are used. These groups are stoppers, bends, hitches, binding knots, and loop knots. *Stoppers* keep a rope from slipping out of a hole or out of the loop of another knot. The knot tied to the end of thread to keep it from slipping out of the needle is a stopper. The *overhand knot*, shown in the diagram on this page, is a kind of stopper. It is easy to tie, but it can jam easily, which makes it hard to untie.

Loop knots are tied to form a loop that is then slipped around something and tightened. The *honda* knot is a loop knot that is used to tie a bowstring to a bow or to make a cowboy's lasso. First tie a loose overhand knot, draw the rope around in a short loop, and bring the rope through the overhand knot. Tie a stopper to the end of your rope to keep it from slipping out.

Binding knots are used to fasten things tightly together or to hold something in place. A binding knot will hold a bundle of things together. It is also used by surgeons for stitching wounds. The *bowknot*, used for tying shoelaces, is a binding knot. The *square knot*, or *reef knot*, is used for many jobs. To make a reef knot, wrap a rope around an object. Take one end of the rope and bend it so that it forms a kind of loop. Take the other end of the rope, draw it through the loop, and over the bottom part of the loop, then bring it back under and through the loop again and pull the knot tight.

Bends are usually used to tie two ropes together. The *sheet bend* is a strong knot that does not slip and is easy to untie. Take two ends of rope, and form one end into a loop as you did for the reef knot. Draw the other end through the loop, bring it around the back of the loop to the front, and then draw it between the two pieces of rope on the right side of the loop. Then pull the knot tight.

Hitches are used to tie a rope onto something. Horse riders use them to tie horses' reins to posts. They are very easy to untie. The *half hitch* is used when you are in a hurry. It is a loose knot that can be untied easily. Throw the rope over something and wrap one end around the other. The *two half hitch*, shown in the diagram, is stronger. Start by making a half hitch and wrap the rope around a second time.

These are just a few simple, basic knots. After you have mastered these, there are many more that you can learn. Your library should have books that illustrate many knots.

KOALA The koala is a woolly, tree-climbing mammal that resembles a teddy bear. It is known also as the Australian bear or native sloth, but in fact it is neither a bear nor a sloth. Koalas live only in Australia, and the

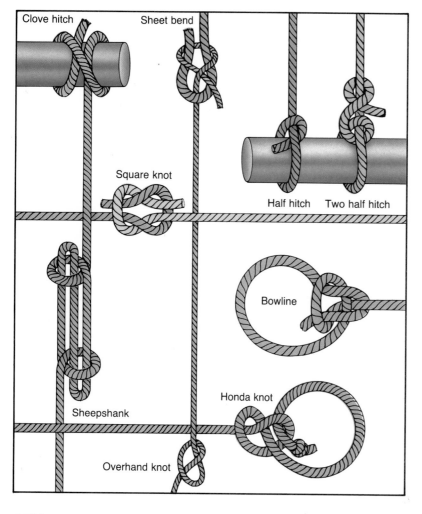

Clove hitch
Sheet bend
Square knot
Half hitch   Two half hitch
Bowline
Sheepshank
Honda knot
Overhand knot

▲ *Although often called a "koala bear," the koala, a marsupial found only in Australia, is not a bear at all.*

females have pouches, like female kangaroos. When a koala is born, it is only three-fourths of an inch (2 cm) long. The newborn koala lives in its mother's pouch until it is six months old and measures about six inches (15 cm) long. It then begins to ride around on its mother's back until it learns to find its own food. Animals that carry their young in pouches this way are called *marsupials*.

The koala has a chubby body covered with gray fur, and it has no tail. Its eyes are small and bright, and its ears are large and bushy. It has a little black, rubbery nose. A full-grown koala weighs about 30 pounds (13.6 kg) and is about the size of a two-year-old child.

Koalas are *nocturnal* (they are awake and active mainly at night). They live in only one kind of tree—the eucalyptus. This is because euca-

lyptus leaves are all the koala ever eats. A koala never drinks water, because it gets all the liquid it needs from the eucalyptus leaves.

Koalas are very shy, and hardly ever leave their trees. This makes them easy to catch. At one time, koalas almost became extinct (disappeared) because hunters were killing them to sell their fur. Now there are laws to protect them.

ALSO READ: AUSTRALIA, AUSTRALIAN MAMMALS, MAMMAL, MARSUPIAL.

KORAN The Koran is the book of holy writings, or scripture, of the faith of *Islam*. People who believe in Islam are known as *Muslims*. They believe that an Arab named Muhammad was chosen to be God's messenger to the world. The word of God was told to Muhammad by the archangel Gabriel in A.D. 610. Muhammad could not read or write, but he repeated what the angel had told him to his followers, who memorized it and wrote it down. These collected writings are called the Koran, which means "reading" in Arabic.

The Koran is divided into 114 chapters, called *surahs*. It contains rules for almost every part of a Mus-

The koala is perhaps the most fussy eater of all the animals. It lives only on the leaves of eucalyptus trees—and only on the leaves of five out of the 350 species of eucalyptus at that!

▼ *This page from the Koran was probably written in the 9th century. The angular script (style of writing) is called Kufic, from the town of Kufah, near Baghdad. Kufah was an important early Islamic center of art and learning.*

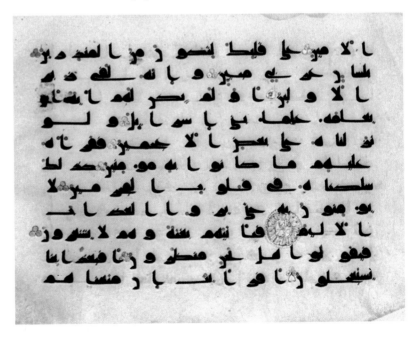

Reverence for the Koran is so great that thousands of Muslims learn it by heart, even though it is almost as long as the Christian New Testament.

lim's life. It teaches that there is only one God, or *Allah*, who created the universe. The Koran says that God sent many prophets, or messengers, to Earth to help people live a better life, and that Muhammad was the last and greatest of these. Some earlier prophets were Abraham, Moses, and Jesus Christ. The Koran tells that everyone will be judged for his or her actions by Allah on the last day. The book includes stories and history that are also found in the Bible. It is read every day in all Muslim schools and *mosques* (temples). One of the holiest things a Muslim can do is to memorize the entire Koran.

ALSO READ: ISLAM, MOSQUE, MUHAMMAD.

KOREA Koreans call their homeland *Choson*, "the land of the morning calm." Their country has been divided into two parts since the end of World War II. North Korea is a Communist country called the People's Democratic Republic of Korea. Its capital is Pyongyang. South Korea is known as the Republic of Korea. Its capital is Seoul. Korea occupies a peninsula slightly larger in area than the state of Kansas. It is in eastern Asia with water on three sides—the Sea of Japan, the Korea Strait, and the Yellow Sea. The Yalu River forms a boundary with China. (See the map with the article on ASIA.)

Much of Korea is very mountainous. Paektu-san (Paektu Peak), 9,003 feet (2,744 m) high, is the highest mountain. Most of the rivers are short and swift-flowing. Korea has no large lakes.

The climate of Korea has sharp regional and seasonal variations. In the northern part of Korea, long, cold winters are common and summers are fairly warm. But in central and southern Korea, winters are brief, and summers are longer and warmer. Most of the country's total rainfall comes between April and November in both the north and south.

About 40 percent of all Koreans earn their living by farming. Chief crops are rice, barley, wheat, sweet potatoes, yams, and soybeans. The rest of the people work in service industries or manufacturing, especially in the north, where there are large steel and textile mills, as well as cement and chemical plants. Other factories in the north turn out rubber products, glass, pottery, and porcelain. Textiles, chemicals, machinery, glass, cement, and steel are manufactured in the south. South Korea's only important mineral deposit is tungsten. Fishing is an important industry in the coastal areas of the country. The forests of North Korea are also a source of income to that region.

The Korean people look rather like the Japanese and Chinese, but are usually taller. The Korean language is similar to Japanese in its grammar,

NORTH KOREA

Capital City: Pyongyang (1,283,000 people).
Area: 46,540 square miles (120,538 sq. km).
Population: 22,000,000.
Government: Communist republic.
Natural Resources: Coal, copper, iron ore, lead, manganese, uranium, zinc.
Export Products: Minerals, metal products, manufactured goods.
Unit of Money: Won.
Official Language: Korean.

SOUTH KOREA

Capital City: Seoul (9,600,000 people).
Area: 38,025 square miles (98,484 sq. km).
Population: 45,200,000.
Government: Republic.
Natural Resources: Tungsten, some coal.
Export Products: Textiles, manufactured goods, footwear, steel, ships.
Unit of Money: Won.
Official Language: Korean.

but the words are different. The Koreans have their own alphabet, but they often use Chinese writing in their literature. Many different religions are practiced in Korea. The oldest religion is *shamanism*, which teaches that there are good spirits and evil spirits in such things as rivers, trees, animals, winds, and fire. Other religions in Korea are Confucianism and Buddhism. They were introduced

▼ *Pusan is South Korea's second largest city. It is also a busy port for fishing and international trade.*

into the country from China over 500 years ago. Christianity was brought to Korea almost 250 years ago.

Korea's powerful neighbors, Japan, China, and Russia have battled for control of the peninsula. In 1910, Japan established Korea as a colony. After World War II, Korea became independent, and Syngman Rhee became president in 1948. Later that year, people living in the northern part of the country formed a Communist government. In 1950, Communist troops from the north invaded the southern part of the country. The fighting that followed became known as the Korean War. After an armistice stopped the fighting in 1953, Korea remained a divided country. Relations between North and South Korea have remained poor. In the 1980s South Korea emerged as a strong economic, industrial and trading country. However, general unrest, including student riots, has left the country politically unstable. South Korea hosted the 1988 Olympic Games.

ALSO READ: ASIA, KOREAN WAR.

KOREAN WAR The main events leading up to the Korean War began at the end of World War II. Korea had been occupied by Japan since 1910. When the war was over, Korea was freed from Japan. Soviet troops occupied North Korea. U.S. troops occupied South Korea. The United Nations said it would be glad to supervise

Many Korean houses have paper windows instead of glass. The paper is strong but only partly transparent. The houses also have paper-covered floors.

The Korean War was one of the fiercest in history. About 1,600,000 Communist troops and 580,000 South Korean and United Nations troops were killed or wounded.

elections throughout Korea in order to establish a single government for the entire country. The Soviet Union refused. So separate elections were held in the north and the south, and two countries were established. Both U.S. troops and Soviet troops withdrew.

On June 25, 1950, the Soviet-trained army of North Korea invaded South Korea by surprise. The South Korean army fell back. The United Nations tried to stop this aggression. The U.N. called on its members to send troops to help South Korea. President Harry S Truman of the United States immediately ordered land, naval, and air forces into Korea. Other countries later helped, but the U.S. and South Korea bore most of the burden. U.S. General Douglas MacArthur became the U.N. supreme commander in Korea.

By the end of July, the North Koreans had pushed the U.N. forces into a small area at the southeastern tip of Korea. But within this area was the important port of Pusan. Meanwhile, U.N. aircraft bombed North Korean tanks and supplies. U.S. troops began arriving at the port. Trying for a quick victory, the North Koreans attacked the area with thousands of soldiers. The defenders held.

On September 15, U.S. Marines came ashore from landing craft at Inchon, farther north on the west coast of Korea, in the same way they had invaded islands held by the Japanese in World War II. The Marines

▲ *U.S. troops await an attack during the Korean War. This war made Korea one of the first crisis areas of the Cold War.*

overcame the North Korean resistance, moved inland, and soon captured the South Korean capital, Seoul. The U.N. troops defending Pusan now broke out. North Koreans surrendered by the thousands. Thousands of others were killed. The rest of them fled to the north.

On October 1, three months after the war began, South Korean troops crossed the 38th parallel dividing North and South Korea. The U.N. force under MacArthur's command pushed far into North Korea to try to unify the country.

North Korea undoubtedly would have fallen, but the Chinese entered the war on North Korea's side. On October 26, a strong Chinese army attacked U.N. forces. Attack followed counterattack in freezing winter weather. By January 1, 1951, the Chinese had pushed U.N. troops back south of the 38th parallel. Seoul fell to the Communists.

Now it was the U.N.'s turn. General Matthew Ridgway launched a counteroffensive that by April had pushed the Chinese north of the parallel once again. The Chinese, badly hurt, wanted a cease-fire. Truce talks began on July 10—a little more than one year after the North Koreans had invaded South Korea.

The truce talks went on for two

▼ *A helicopter is used to fly a wounded U.S. soldier away from the battlefield during the Korean War.*

years. The fighting continued, but the battle line moved little. On July 27, 1953, an agreement was reached to end the Korean War. A buffer zone 2½ miles (4 km) wide was laid out between North Korea and South Korea. No troops from either side could go into this zone.

ALSO READ: KOREA; MACARTHUR, DOUGLAS.

KRAKATOA   see VOLCANO.

KREMLIN   In the center of Moscow stands a magnificent group of brightly colored buildings topped with tall spires and golden domes and surrounded by a high stone wall. This is the famous 500-year-old Kremlin. "Kremlin" comes from the Russian word *kreml'*, meaning "fortress." Many Russian cities are built around a kremlin.

The wall around Moscow's Kremlin is a mile and a half (2.4 km) long and as tall as 70 feet (21 m) in some places. Twenty towers rise above the wall. Many of the buildings inside the wall are joined by underground passageways. The buildings were constructed at various times over several centuries, dating back to the late Middle Ages.

The Grand Kremlin Palace, built between 1838 and 1849, has the most imposing buildings within the Kremlin. It was the home of the Russian *czars* (kings) until the last, Nicholas II, was killed by revolutionaries in 1918. The throne-room of the palace is now the meeting place of the Supreme Soviet (legislative assembly of the Soviet Union).

Several picturesque golden-domed cathedrals are also in the Kremlin. Like many other churches in the Soviet Union, they have been turned into museums. They contain priceless paintings, jewels, and czarist crowns. Another Kremlin landmark

is the Tower of Ivan the Great, a bell tower 320 feet (97.5 m) high. Near the tower is the Czar's Bell, the largest bell in the world. It is 20 feet (6 m) high and weighs nearly 200 tons (181 metric tons)!

The Soviet Palace of Congresses is the newest building in the Kremlin. The modern glass and steel structure is often the site of concerts, operas, and ballets.

ALSO READ: MOSCOW, RUSSIAN HISTORY, SOVIET UNION.

KUWAIT   The tiny nation of Kuwait is one of the richest countries in the world. It lies at the northwestern tip of the Persian Gulf.

Kuwait's growth and prosperity depends on oil. Apart from the capital city of Kuwait the country is almost all desert. The climate is hot.

In 1990, a dispute about oil arose between Kuwait and neighboring Iraq. Saddam Hussein, the president of Iraq, ordered his armies to invade Kuwait. A few weeks later he proclaimed it annexed as a province of Iraq. The United Nations protested the invasion, and the United States and other countries sent forces to Saudi Arabia to stop Iraq from attacking that country too.

ALSO READ: ARABIA, IRAQ.

▲ *The Kremlin is the old center of Moscow, the capital of the Soviet Union. Its walls and towers rise from a hill on the left bank of the Moskva River.*

In Kuwait, the average income per person is higher than in the United States. Kuwait also has as many doctors per head of population as the United States.

After Iraq invaded Kuwait, the United Nations imposed economic sanctions on Iraq in an attempt to force Saddam Hussein's troops out of Kuwait. After five months, the sanctions showed no signs of accomplishing their objective, and international forces, under the leadership of the United States, attacked Iraq by air on January 16, 1991, behind a United Nations flag.

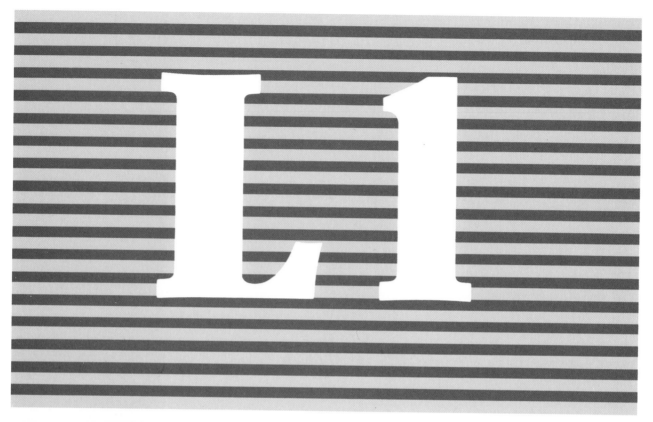

▲ *Samuel Gompers, first president of the American Federation of Labor.*

LABOR UNION One worker alone often finds it very difficult to obtain better working conditions. But when many workers join together in a group to ask their employer for the same thing, they can more easily get what they want. "Labor" is a term for working people as a group. When working people join together to form an organized group to obtain better working conditions, the group is called a labor union.

The idea of labor unions began in Europe in the Middle Ages. People skilled in a particular kind of work formed organizations called *guilds* in order to obtain aid and protection. Great changes occurred in England and the United States in the 1700's and 1800's during the Industrial Revolution. Time-saving machinery was invented and large factories were built. Manufacturing and mining industries were developed. Many people went to work in the factories and the mines. They were usually forced to live in crowded, unsanitary housing near their jobs. They were paid low wages, and working conditions were often harsh and dangerous. Workers rebelled against this unjust treatment, and formed the first labor unions to obtain improved working conditions. The first labor unions in the United States were started by shoemakers and carpenters in Philadelphia about 1790. Soon workers in other trades formed unions.

There are two kinds of labor unions. People doing the same kind of work (e.g., carpenters) belong to *craft unions*. All the people working in the same industry, no matter what their job is, belong to an *industrial union*. For example, members of the United Auto Workers of America might be welders, painters, or electricians, but they all work in the auto industry.

Single, or local, unions often join together to form national unions. In 1886, the craft unions throughout the United States joined together to become the American Federation of Labor (AFL), the first successful collection of different unions. In 1938, the industrial unions became the Congress of Industrial Organizations (CIO). These two groups merged in 1955 to form the AFL-CIO.

The growth of labor unions was marked by much bloodshed. In the early days, workers' demonstrations were often cruelly suppressed. Some were put to death for crimes they probably did not commit. The workers themselves often used violence when nobody would listen to their requests. But today, labor and management (company owners) try to talk to one another in a process called *collective bargaining*. Both unions and management have representatives who meet to discuss the workers' demands. They try to reach a fair decision. Sometimes a third party, or *mediator*, not involved in the argument, tries to help them agree. If this does not work, unions may *go on strike* (stop working). When thousands of workers throughout the country go on strike to aid each other, entire industries can be stopped. When a group of workers whose services are considered to be needed for the public's safety, such as fire fighters, go on strike, the employer can obtain a court *injunction*. This forces the workers to return to their jobs. If they don't, they or their leaders may be fined or jailed.

Early labor unions had simple demands: shorter work weeks, higher wages, and safer working conditions. Now unions ask for health and welfare benefits, paid holidays, insurance, and many other side, or *fringe*, benefits. Labor unions in the United States have become very important in politics. Millions of workers can have tremendous influence on an election, because many of them will vote for the candidate who promises to do the most for workers. Also, labor unions have political action funds—often large sums of money they give to the campaign funds of candidates they back. Many of the aims of labor unions have been achieved. U.S. workers, for example, are among the

highest paid in the world.

ALSO READ: CHILD LABOR, GUILD.

▲ *A certificate of membership in the Brotherhood of Locomotive Engineers.*

LABRADOR see NEWFOUNDLAND-LABRADOR.

LACE Lace is a delicate open fabric, woven of silk, cotton, linen, nylon, or other thread. Clothing decorated with lace was very fashionable in Europe among wealthy people during the 1500's, 1600's, and 1700's. Rich people wore lace collars, lace sleeves, and even shoe decorations made of lace. Women often wore lace scarves. (In Spain, where these scarves are still worn, they are called

▲ *The finest lace is still made by hand. The work requires skill and patience.*

Lace decorations worn around the neck (called ruffs) were very popular during the reign of Queen Elizabeth I. Ruffs grew so large that people had to use spoons with extra-long handles to avoid crushing their ruffs while eating.

mantillas.) Men often had lace cuffs on their trousers, and some wealthy women even wore dresses made entirely of lace.

Today, lace is not quite so popular as it once was. Men rarely wear it at all. But lace is still widely used for women's underclothing, formal dresses, handkerchiefs, scarves, tablecloths, and curtains.

Lace was first made in Italy in the 1400's. Other countries later developed their own styles of lace-making. Belgium, Italy, France, Spain, Ireland, England, and Flanders all became centers of fine lace-making. Laces became fancier and more costly as years passed. Some laces were made of gold and silver threads.

The two main types of handmade lace are *needlepoint lace* and *bobbin lace*, or *pillow lace*. Needlepoint lace is made with a needle and thread and a piece of parchment or paper backed with cloth. The design for the lace is first drawn on the parchment, and heavy stitches are made in the parchment around the border of the design. These border stitches are used as the base for the design stitches. Aside from these stitches, the lace-maker never sews through the parchment. He or she attaches the design stitches to the border stitches. When the lace is done, the parchment is removed by cutting the border stitches.

Bobbin lace is made with several

spools, or bobbins, of thread and a long stuffed pad, or pillow. The design is drawn on parchment, and pins are stuck through the parchment, along the lines of the design, into the pillow. The threads of the bobbins are looped around the pins and then passed under, over, or around each other, so that the threads are woven into delicate designs. When the lace is done, it is removed by pulling out the pins.

Most lace today is made by machine. An English manufacturer made the first machine lace in the late 1700's. The bobbin net machine, invented by John Heathcoat of England in 1809, was able to make patterned net that looked very much like handmade Brussels lace. Heathcoat's invention was the model for today's lace-making machines. Machine-made lace can be produced much more quickly and more cheaply than handmade lace, but fine handmade lace is still made all over the world.

ALSO READ: NEEDLEWORK.

LACROSSE When the French pioneers first settled in eastern Canada, they saw the Indians playing a strange game. The Indians tossed a small ball of stuffed leather back and forth with long-handled sticks. The sticks were crooked and had nets at the top. To the French, the sticks resembled a cross, so they called the game *la crosse*.

Lacrosse is a popular sport in the United States, Canada, and other countries. It was adopted as the national game of Canada in 1867. For many years, lacrosse in the United States was played only on the East Coast, but it is now popular in many other parts of the country.

Lacrosse players must be fast runners and must be able to throw and catch the ball skillfully with their lacrosse sticks. A lacrosse stick (*crosse*) is made of either hickory wood or fiberglass, and is 4 to 6 feet (1.2–1.8 m) in length. A triangular net made of strings of leather is attached to the end of the stick. The lacrosse ball is made of hard rubber.

A U.S. men's lacrosse team has 10 players—a *goalkeeper*, three *defensemen*, three *attackmen*, and three *midfielders*. (A Canadian men's team has 12 players; a U.S. women's team has 12, too.) The field is 110 yards (100 m) long and 60 yards (55 m) wide. It is divided in half by a *center line*. Six-foot-high (1.8 m) and wide cone-shaped nets are placed at opposite ends of the field.

The object of a lacrosse game is for one team to score more goals than the other. A goal, which counts one point, is scored when a player uses the crosse to throw the ball past the other team's goalkeeper and into the net. A game is usually divided into four 15-minute quarters.

Lacrosse players use their sticks and bodies to prevent the other team's players from coming within shooting distance of their goalkeeper. Players may hit the stick of a ball-carrier in order to knock the ball loose, but they cannot hit the ball-carrier on the head, arms, or body. Players, except for the goalkeeper, cannot touch the ball with their hands. In many ways, lacrosse is like ice hockey. Because

▼ *In women's lacrosse, world championships have been won by the United States in 1982 and Australia in 1986.*

lacrosse is a rough game, the players often wear protective equipment.

LAFAYETTE, MARQUIS DE (1757–1834)

A wealthy French nobleman became one of the greatest heroes of the American Revolution. Marie Joseph Paul Ives Roch Gilbert Motier, Marquis de Lafayette, was born in Chavaniac, France. He entered the French army at 14, and had risen to the rank of captain by the time he was 19 years old!

When the American colonies declared their independence, Lafayette offered to serve in the Continental Army without pay. By a special resolution of the Continental Congress, he was commissioned as a major general in the army. He was then 20.

Lafayette was placed on General Washington's staff, and served with distinction in several battles. He also gave much of his own fortune to help the colonies. In 1825, Congress granted him almost 12,000 acres (4,860 hectares) of land in Louisiana.

Upon his return to France, Lafayette played a leading role in the French Revolution. He became a member of the French National Assembly, commander of the French National Guard, and helped to write the French Bill of Rights. When he opposed the violence of the French rebels, he was declared a traitor, his property was taken, and he was exiled. He fled from France. But he was arrested abroad as a leader of the Revolution and imprisoned.

In 1799, he returned to France. He had little to do with politics because he disapproved of the policies of Napoleon Bonaparte, who was by that time leader of the French government. But for the rest of his life, Lafayette fought for social equality, religious tolerance, and freedom of the press in France.

ALSO READ: AMERICAN REVOLUTION, FRENCH REVOLUTION.

The game of lacrosse as played by the Indians had few, if any, rules. Sometimes hundreds of players took part and the game ranged over miles of territory.

▲ *The Marquis de Lafayette, French soldier and statesman, and a hero of the American Revolution.*

▲ *Jean de La Fontaine, the French poet who took the fables of earlier writers, such as Aesop, and turned them into verse.*

▼ *Lake Titicaca, on the border of Peru and Bolivia, South America, is the world's highest large lake. It is 12,497 feet (3,809 m) above sea level.*

LAFFITE, JEAN see PIRATES AND PRIVATEERS.

LA FONTAINE, JEAN DE (1621–1695) The famous French poet, Jean de La Fontaine, is best known for his imaginary stories, or fables. La Fontaine was born in Chateau-Thierry, France. He was educated as a priest and as a lawyer. But he later became a writer. His first literary work was the *Contes et nouvelles en vers*, a book of stories told in verse.

His *Fables* were written later, in three groups, between 1668 and 1694. They were based mainly on the fables of the ancient Greek writer, Aesop. The fables are stories about animals that speak and behave like people. Each story has a moral, or teaches a lesson about life. La Fontaine retold Aesop's fables in verse and added wise and amusing comments of his own. "The Fox and the Grapes," "The Grasshopper and the Ant," and "The Lion and the Mouse" are a few of these tales.

The fable of "The Fox and the Crow" tells how unwise it is to listen to flatterers. The crow found a large piece of cheese one day, and flew up into a tree to eat it. The fox, who wanted the cheese, sat under the tree and told the crow what a beautiful voice it had. "Let me hear you sing but one song," the fox said. When the crow opened its beak to caw, the piece of cheese fell to the ground and was gobbled up by the fox.

Although La Fontaine wrote his *Fables* for adults, children everywhere have enjoyed them ever since. His works brought him great fame during his lifetime, and he enjoyed the financial help and encouragement of several noble and wealthy patrons.

ALSO READ: AESOP, FABLE.

LAKE Have you ever watched puddles form in the street when it rains? The rainwater collects in low places in the pavement. Lakes are formed in a similar way. Water collects in large *depressions* (hollows) on the surface of the Earth. The depressions fill either with rainwater or with the water that flows from rivers, mountain streams, or underground springs.

Many of the world's lakes lie in regions where huge *glaciers* (masses of slowly moving ice) moved across the land during the last cold period of the ice age, which ended about 10,000 years ago. The glaciers carved hollows in the land as they traveled. These hollows filled with water when the glaciers melted. In Minnesota there are many lakes formed in this way.

Lakes are formed in other ways,

SOME INTERESTING LAKES

LAKE COMO, a lake formed by the action of glaciers, is one of the most beautiful lakes in the world. It is located in northern Italy at the foot of the Alps, the largest mountain system in Europe. Its shores are lined with magnificent homes and gardens.

LOCH NESS, in northern Scotland, is thought by some people to be the home of a monster 20–60 feet (6–18 m) long. They say that perhaps a family of prehistoric animals has survived in the loch's (lake's) deep, icy waters for millions of years.

LAKE SUPERIOR, one of the five Great Lakes of North America, is the largest freshwater lake in the world. It covers about 31,800 square miles (82,400 sq. km).

THE CASPIAN SEA is the largest saltwater lake in the world. It covers about 143,630 square miles (370,000 sq. km). It is located in the Soviet Union and Iran.

LAKE TITICACA lies at the highest level above the sea of any large lake in the world. It is located 12,497 feet (3,809 m) above sea level on the border between Peru and Bolivia.

MANITOU LAKE has an area of 42 square miles (109 sq. km). It is the world's largest "lake within a lake." It is located on Manitoulin Island in Lake Huron.

too. Crater Lake in southwestern Oregon lies in the *crater* (bowl-shaped opening) of an *extinct* volcano. (An extinct volcano is one that no longer erupts.) Crater Lake is not connected with any rivers or streams. Melting snow keeps it full. Lakes are also formed when the Earth's *crust* (outer layer) shifts and cracks. Water fills the crack. Lake Baikal (or Baykal) in the Soviet Union began in this way. It is the world's deepest lake.

Another kind of lake is the *sinkhole lake*, which is found in limestone regions. Limestone is a kind of soft rock that dissolves in water. Rainwater slowly wears a depression in the rock, and the depression fills with water. Northern Florida has many sinkhole lakes.

Some lakes are called "seas," although they are not connected with the oceans. The Caspian Sea in the Soviet Union and the Dead Sea between Israel and Jordan are saltwater lakes. Saltwater lakes are fed by rivers and streams, but they have no outlets. Water can leave these lakes only by evaporation. The Sea of Galilee in Israel is a freshwater lake. The Jordan River passes through it, bringing water in at one end and carrying it out at the other.

Artificial lakes can be made by

▲ *High in the Rocky Mountains, in the Banff National Park, Alberta, Canada, is Lake Moraine. Its waters come from melting glaciers and mountain streams.*

building dams across rivers. The river water backs up behind the dam, and a lake is formed. A new lake, called Lake Powell, was created in Arizona in 1963 behind Glen Canyon Dam, which blocks the Colorado River. Both natural and man-made lakes are useful to people. Canals can be built to bring water from lakes to irrigate farmlands. Lakes can also be used as *reservoirs* (areas for storing drinking water). And lakes provide fun for people—fishing, boating, swimming, and water-skiing.

In the future, new lakes will form, and the lakes that exist today will disappear. Some will be filled in little by little with bits of sand or earth carried by rivers and streams. Others may slowly dry up because of a change in climate or because the streams that feed them dry up.

ALSO READ: ARAL SEA; CASPIAN SEA; DAM; DEAD SEA; FOOD WEB; GALILEE, SEA OF; GLACIER; GREAT LAKES; GREAT SALT LAKE; ICE AGE; VOLCANO.

▼ *Lake Kariba is on the border of Zimbabwe and Zambia in Africa. The Kariba dam in Zimbabwe provides water for the dry season.*

Lakes sometimes form inside the craters of extinct volcanoes. Crater Lake in Oregon is 1,930 feet (588 m) deep and lies at the top of an ancient volcano.

▲ *Houses are built on stilts in coastal lagoons of Benin, a small nation in West Africa. People move about in canoes and other boats.*

LAKE DWELLERS In very ancient times, many people began to build their houses over water. They did this is order to escape their enemies—wild animals or other people. Lake dwellers seem to have existed as long as 1½ million years ago. Two kinds of lake dwellings were built. People made mounds of stone, brush, or mud, in the water. They drove short *pilings* (heavy pieces of wood) into the mounds and built houses on the pilings. On stormier lakes, they made stronger bases for the pilings by placing square log frames on the lake bottom. They would drive long poles into the lake bottom within these frames, and then build their houses on these long poles. The lake dwellers had to climb ladders to get into their houses. They would pull the ladders up after them, so that no enemy could follow. By living on the water, the lake dwellers were able to use more of the good land around a lake for farming. People could even go fishing without leaving their home!

When people began to use bronze and iron tools, they were able to build larger, stronger houses. In Switzerland's lakes, people have found ruins of large, well-built lake communities. Even today, some groups of people—such as those in the Philippine Islands and along the Amazon River in South America—still live in houses built over the waters of lakes.

ALSO READ: ANTHROPOLOGY, STONE AGE.

▲ *Charles Lamb, the English writer. He and his sister Mary wrote the famous* Tales from Shakespeare.

LAMB, CHARLES (1775–1834) Charles Lamb was a popular British writer of essays and poetry. He is also known for the book, *Tales from Shakespeare* (1807), which he wrote with his elder sister, Mary (1764–1847). In this book the stories of Shakespeare's plays are retold in simple language for children. Mary wrote the comedies, and he the tragedies.

Lamb was born in London, England. At age 17 he went to work as a clerk in the East India House of London. He stayed there until he retired in 1825. Lamb's life was a tragic one, but he was helped by his many friends and admirers. His sister suffered from fits of insanity all her life—she killed their mother in 1796. Lamb took care of Mary when she was not in an institution. He never married.

Lamb's writings included many poems, articles, and criticisms of plays, but his witty, amusing essays brought him his greatest fame. Most were written under his pen name, "Elia." One of his best liked and funniest essays was "A Dissertation Upon Roast Pig." This essay tells how a farm caught fire one day and all the farmer's pigs were burned. The farmer touched one of the pigs and scorched his fingers. He put his fingers in his mouth and became the first person to discover the sweet taste of roast pork. Soon lots of farmers were burning their farms down so that they could enjoy roast pork!

ALSO READ: CHILDREN'S LITERATURE.

LAMP see LIGHTING.

LAMPREY see FISH.

LANGLEY, SAMUEL see SMITHSONIAN INSTITUTION.

LANGUAGE ARTS Civilization is built on language—on people's ability to communicate and understand. For this reason, and others, language is one of the most important skills that people develop. *Language arts* is the study of how to use language effectively. In the language arts, you learn how to express your ideas so that others will understand you. And you also learn how to listen and read so that you will understand other people's ideas.

The language arts include listening, speaking, reading, and writing. All of these are skills that you learn by practice. You learn them by *doing* them. When you were a baby, you first learned to talk by listening carefully to the words used by people around you. Then you tried to imitate (copy) those words yourself.

Listening and speaking skills go together. When a person speaks, there must be someone to listen; otherwise there is no communication. A good listener must be able to concentrate on (pay attention to) the speaker's words. He must be able to follow the speaker's ideas and sort out the important parts of the message from the unimportant parts. A listener must also pay attention to the speaker's "tone of voice." The tone of voice tells you the speaker's feelings or the mood of his or her message. A good listener, by understanding more, gets more enjoyment from what he or she hears. A good listener will enjoy a movie more than a bad listener, who may miss some of the dialogue and not understand what is happening on the screen.

Speaking well means sending messages so that listeners will understand them. You may have a brilliant idea in your mind, but if you jumble up the message, people will have a hard time understanding what your idea is. Good speaking also means being sure you don't bore your listeners. Bored people don't really listen. A good speaker must consider the listener. For example, a baby or younger child will not understand you if you use big words. A speaker should be able to give information clearly, accurately, and without wasting words. For example, if you give your classmates directions for a science experiment, you must give each step in order, stated clearly so your classmates will know exactly what to do.

Reading and writing skills go together, just as listening and speaking skills do. The writer sends a message for the reader to receive. Like a listener, a reader must learn to follow the writer's ideas and sort out the important ideas from the less important ones. He or she must also pay attention to the "tone of voice," or the mood, of the written message. An important part of the reading skill is learning to enjoy reading. Good readers read not only for information, but for the pleasure they can get from reading all types of writing.

Writing means sending messages in written form so that readers will understand them. You begin to write by learning how to form the alphabet letters and arranging them to spell words. As you learn to spell words, you practice arranging them on paper so that they form messages that others can understand. Just like a speaker, a writer must present ideas clearly and accurately and must try not to bore his or her readers. A writer must also consider who the readers will be. You probably wouldn't write a story or article the same way for adult readers as you would for small children.

By learning to communicate well through listening, speaking, reading, and writing, you can understand others better and help them to understand you. You also learn about the world by communicating with language. If people send and receive unclear, jumbled-up messages, no one will learn very much and civilization will not progress very far. This is why the language arts are taught all through school.

Television, telephones, and computers make good listening and reading very important. They provide gigantic amounts of information. The language arts teach you to read and listen for important information, and then take care of it quickly before more information piles up. You also gain skills that help you understand a

▲ *Henry Kissinger, former U.S. diplomat and government advisor, is a busy public speaker at colleges, institutions and business meetings. Public speaking is an important language art. Good public speakers keep their audiences interested and persuade people to a point of view.*

Sports commentators can speak more than 300 words per minute continuously without losing their clarity and becoming unintelligible.

LANGUAGES

It has been calculated that there are more people learning English in China than the total population of the United States.

There are more than half a million different words in some English dictionaries. Most of us use less than ten thousand words.

good novel or poem and help you enjoy a play.

Through language arts, you learn to develop and improve your writing and speaking skills. You learn to give speeches, argue in debates, and participate in panel discussions. You learn to create stories, poetry, advertisements, reports, letters, and other forms of writing. You even study the English language itself. You learn about its history and about the way it works. Language arts involves dramatics, too—everything from easy pantomimes to big stage plays.

■ LEARN BY DOING

Imagine a friend does not know how to tie his or her shoelaces. Write a letter to him or her describing exactly how it is done. You will find it is not as easy to explain as you may have thought! You will have to write very carefully and to *think hard* about what you are writing. ■

For further information on:

General, *see* ADVERTISING, BOOK, COMMUNICATION, ENGLISH LANGUAGE, GRAMMAR, LANGUAGES, MAGAZINE, NEWSPAPER, PARTS OF SPEECH, RADIO BROADCASTING, TELEVISION BROADCASTING, WORD GAMES.
Listening, *see* HEARING.
Reading, *see* AUTOBIOGRAPHY, BIOGRAPHY, CHILDREN'S LITERATURE, FAIRY TALE, LEGEND, LITERATURE, NOVEL, POETRY, SCIENCE FICTION, SHORT STORY.
Speaking, *see* DEBATING, DRAMA, PRONUNCIATION, PUBLIC SPEAKING, SPEECH.
Writing, *see* ALPHABET, CAPITALIZATION, FIGURES OF SPEECH, HANDWRITING, JOURNALISM, LETTER WRITING, PICTURE WRITING, PUNCTUATION, SPELLING, WRITTEN LANGUAGE.

LANGUAGES Suppose a baby shipwrecked alone on a desert island were able to live and grow. Would he or she be able to speak in a language that another person could under-

stand? The child would have *ideas*, but he or she would be unlikely to have words to express these ideas. If the child remained alone on the desert island, he or she would probably never feel the need to express them.

But suppose one day another person appeared on the beach. The child would certainly then feel the need for expressing thoughts, for being understood, and for understanding the other person. The two could probably communicate through grunts or signs. They could express friendship, and by making signs toward their mouths they could show hunger. But how could one ask the other, "How long have you been here?" They would need a common language.

What is a language? It is a system used by human beings for communicating through words. Animals are known to communicate with one another in various ways, but not through words, although dolphins and some types of whales may use languages. But, for the time being, we can say that language is a characteristic only of human beings.

About 90 percent of all human communication takes place through spoken language. Wherever there are people, there is language. Even the most primitive people speak a language of some kind.

Development of Language A language can be spoken or written. In most cases, spoken language develops before written language. People will make up a system of talking to one another through words. They will agree upon different names for different things and ways of expressing different actions. A very long time may then pass before they invent a way of writing. To make up even the simplest language is not easy. For instance, how would you express the fact that something is big? The Araucanian Indians of Chile solved this problem by doubling the name of something big. They call one of their rivers the "Calle Calle River." Its name is Calle, and because it is very wide and long, they say the name twice!

Some languages never become written languages. The Inca Indians, who established a vast empire high up in the Andean mountains of South America, spoke their own language, *Quechua*. But, as far as we know, it was never written down.

If you study any language, you will see in it a clear reflection of the people who speak it, their surroundings, and their history. For instance, the Arabic language has many different ways of saying the word for "camel." This is because the life of the Arabs has always been closely connected with this animal. They eat its meat, drink its milk, and use it for transportation and as an article of trade.

Whenever a language is preserved, even if it is only a few words, future generations can find out something about the people who spoke it. Wherever people go, they take their language with them. Scholars can trace the movements of peoples in the past by words that have passed from one language into another. As people change and develop, so do languages. Think of the space program. Were there names in the English language for all the different kinds of inventions and mechanisms that came into existence so that human beings could venture into space? Obviously not. An official in the space program says that many technical words were coined (made up) from Greek or Latin roots (words), but quite a lot of others have come from slang and engineering jargon (specialized language). *Exosphere, parametric receiver,* and *photosphere* are some examples of words made up from Greek and Latin. *Bird* (for rocket), *brain* (for guidance system), and *scrub* (for cancellation of mission) are examples of slang or jargon. These words are now part of the English language. This is just *one* example of how a language

expands, borrowing words and making up others as new needs arise.

Languages also die. Civilizations break up, nations are conquered by others, and in many cases people pick up the language of the conquering nation and stop using their own in daily conversation. Classical Greek and Latin, once major European languages, are now written and spoken by few people.

THE FAMILY OF LANGUAGES

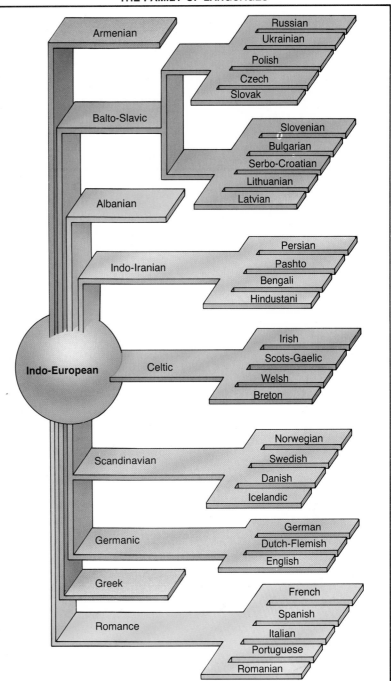

▲ *The most widely-spoken languages belong to the Indo-European group. The diagram shows many of the Indo-European tongues that originated in Europe, the U.S.S.R., southwestern Asia, and in India. Some Indo-European languages have spread around the world.*

LANGUAGES

▲ *Signs in both English and Chinese crowd a busy shopping street in Hong Kong. Many places have dual languages.*

The language spoken by the common people of the Roman Empire (Vulgar Latin) was quite unlike classical Latin. It was spoken by people who could neither read nor write and who had learned Latin by ear. It was from this Vulgar Latin that the Italian, French, and Spanish languages grew.

■ LEARN BY DOING

We saw that words pass from language to language. Look in a French dictionary (if you do not have one, use your library). You will find many words that are the same, or very like, English words. Now look in a German dictionary. You will find far fewer words that are the same as English words. What do you find if you look in a Spanish dictionary? ■

Today's Languages How many languages exist today? It is extremely difficult to pinpoint the exact number, but some scholars have counted about 4,000. The languages of the world have been divided into several families by scholars of *linguistics* (the study of language—its sounds and its changes).

The main language families are Indo-European; Hamito–Semitic (these include languages of the Middle East such as Arabic, Hebrew, and Aramaic); Ural-Altaic (Finnish, Turkish, and some others); Japanese and Korean; Sino-Tibetan (Chinese, Thai, and Burmese); Dravidian (languages of southern India); Malayo-Polynesian (spoken in the extensive area of the South Pacific). There are three African language families: Khoisan (Click), Nilo–Saharian, and Niger–Kordofanian. American Indian languages can be roughly divided into more than 100 families. A few languages do not seem to belong to any family; for example, that of the Ainu of Japan.

Scholars believe that the languages of the Indo-European family, today spoken by about half the people of the world, have all come from one common and very ancient "mother" language spoken in central Europe around 4000 B.C. Certain words, such as those for "mother" and "father," are similar in all the Indo-European languages. Branches of this extensive family range from the Hindustani language of India to the languages spoken in Russia. They include almost all the languages of Europe.

Two branches of the Indo-European language family are of particular interest—the Romance and the Germanic languages of Europe. Latin has been the most important influence on the Romance languages, which are Italian, French, Spanish, Portuguese, and Romanian. Languages grouped in the Germanic branch include English, German, and Dutch-Flemish. Related to the Germanic branch are the Scandinavian languages, Danish, Norwegian, Icelandic, and Swedish. All these languages are spoken in a densely populated region of the world. They have been greatly influenced by wars of conquest, shifts of population, inventions, and changing fashions. Linguists trace the passage of thousands of words from one language to another, particularly in the Germanic and Romance branches. The word "elephant" is an example of how a word can travel through many languages, changing on the way. Linguists believe the word was originally "elpend" and was an Egyptian word. In ancient times, it traveled from Egyptian to Greek ("elephas"), and then to Latin ("elephantus"). From Latin, it went into the French language ("olifant"), and was then borrowed by Old English ("elifaunt"). Since then the English spelling has changed to become the word we know today—elephant.

Persons must know two or more languages well to *translate* (say the same thing in another language) written or spoken words. Translators must have a thorough knowledge of the grammar, vocabulary, and syntax (word order) of the languages they use. They should also know the languages' *idioms* (characteristic expressions peculiar to a language) in order to translate *meaning* rather than just *words*. For example, the U.S. expression "no skin off my nose" makes no sense to a French person when translated word for word.

Expert interpreters can become *simultaneous translators*. They translate words as soon as they are spoken. The United Nations uses simultaneous translators to make speeches understandable to all its members.

Several "universal languages" have recently been invented, so that people all over the world might understand one another. Some of these are Esperanto, Interlingua, Volapük, and Novial. But none has been completely successful.

Also recently invented are computer languages. There are two types: the language the computer uses inside itself (*machine code*), and the language used to program it, which is easier for human beings to learn.

For further information on:

Ancient Languages, *see* GREEK, LATIN.

How Languages are Spoken, *see* HEARING, PRONUNCIATION, SPEECH, VOCABULARY.

How Languages are Written, *see* ALPHABET, DICTIONARY, FIGURES OF SPEECH, GRAMMAR, PICTURE WRITING, SPELLING.

Languages Used Today, *see* ARABIC; CHINESE; COMPUTER; ENGLISH LANGUAGE; GERMAN LANGUAGE; HEBREW; INDIANS, AMERICAN; ROMANCE LANGUAGES; RUSSIAN; SCANDINAVIAN LANGUAGES; YIDDISH.

The Study of Languages, *see* LANGUAGE ARTS, READING.

What Languages are Used for, *see* COMMUNICATIONS, LITERATURE.

LAOS In Laos you can sometimes see elephants walking along a city street. Laos is known as the "Land of a Million Elephants." It is a landlocked country in Southeast Asia. China and Burma lie to the north; Vietnam is to the east; Thailand to the west; and Kampuchea (Cambodia) to the south. Laos is about twice the size of the state of Pennsylvania. The country's capital and largest city is Vientiane on the Mekong River, about 130 miles (209 km) south of the old royal capital of Luang Prabang. (See the map with the article on ASIA.)

Most of Laos is covered with jungles, forests, and mountains. The Mekong River flows through the western part of the country. It is Laos's major transportation route.

The climate is affected by the tropical monsoons. These winds bring warm rains from May to October. Between November and February, Laos is cool and dry. During the rest of the year, it is hot and dry.

Most Laotians earn their living by farming. Rice is the most important crop. Other agricultural products are cotton, tobacco, fruits and vegetables, poppies for opium production, sugarcane, and coffee. The forests contain many valuable trees, including teak. Wood-processing is the country's main industry. Laos has no railroads and few good roads. Airplanes are sometimes the only way to move things.

Most Laotian people practice the

Laos is a very poor country, with only one doctor for about every 20,000 people and two telephones for every 1,000 people.

LAOS

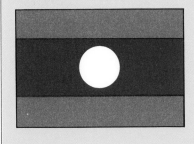

Capital City: Vientiane (120,000 people).
Area: 91,429 square miles (236,800 sq. km).
Population: 3,900,000.
Government: Communist republic.
Natural Resources: Tin, forests.
Export Products: Hydroelectric power, lumber, coffee, tin concentrates.
Unit of Money: Kip.
Official Language: Lao.

The Lapps are among the smallest people in Europe. Many of them are only about 5 feet (1.5 m) tall. They are, however, strong and muscular.

▼ *A Lapp with his reindeer. Many Lapps still follow the migrating reindeer herds as they move about northern Sweden.*

Buddhist religion. Life in the villages often centers on the temples where many festivals are held.

At one time, much of Laos was part of Thailand, but the French gained control of it in the late 1800's. The country was part of French Indochina until 1949, when it gained independence, although remaining within the French Union. The Pathet Lao (pro-communist party) waged war within the country from 1953 to 1974. U.S. forces and Thai mercenaries fought on the side of the government. Communist North Vietnam supported the Pathet Lao. The Pathet Lao signed a ceasefire and ruled with the Vientiane government until 1975, when the coalition was upset by the communist takeover of South Vietnam and Kampuchea. The Pathet Lao gained full control of Laos. The old constitutional monarchy was abolished, and a Lao People's Democratic Republic was established, with Prince Souphanouvong as president.

ALSO READ: ASIA, INDOCHINA.

LAPLAND Lapland, the home of the Lapps, is not a nation but a bleak, barren region of Europe, north of the Arctic Circle. It covers the northern parts of Norway, Sweden, and Finland, and the northwestern part of the Soviet Union.

The Lapps are a short, fair-skinned people. They speak a language similar to Finnish and Hungarian. Only about 35,000 Lapps live in Lapland today. Some herd reindeer, just as their ancestors did for centuries. Reindeer pull sleds over snow and ice and serve as pack animals. Their hides are used to make clothes and tents. The herders also get meat, milk, and cheese from the reindeer. Reindeer feed on mosses and lichens, because very little else grows in this cold region.

After an accident at a nuclear power station in the Soviet Union in 1986, radioactive particles fell on the plants in Lapland. Many reindeer absorbed these poisonous substances and became dangerous to eat. Experts estimated that perhaps one-third of the reindeer will have to be killed between 1986 and 1991.

Herders who move from place to place are called *nomads*. All Lapp families were once nomads. Now most Lapps have settled in small fishing and farming villages, or work in Lapland's rich iron mines.

ALSO READ: FINLAND, LICHEN, NORWAY, SOVIET UNION, SWEDEN.

LARVA see METAMORPHOSIS.

LA SALLE, SIEUR DE (1643–1687) The first European to sail down the Mississippi River to the Gulf of Mexico was a French explorer, Robert Cavelier, later called La Salle. Born in Rouen, France, he was trained to be a Jesuit missionary. But in 1666, La Salle emigrated to Canada, where he became a fur trader. La Salle made many explorations across the northeastern wilderness of North America, and became familiar with the languages and customs of the Indians. La Salle claimed to have discovered the Ohio River in 1671.

In 1674, La Salle was sent to France as a representative of the French colonial governor to obtain permission to build Fort Frontenac, a trading station at the mouth of the St. Lawrence River. His mission was successful. He not only received command of the fort, but also a title, Sieur de (Lord of) La Salle.

In 1679, La Salle sailed up the St. Lawrence to near where the city of Buffalo, New York, now stands. There his men built a ship called the *Griffon* to sail on the Great Lakes to Lake Michigan. In 1680, La Salle built Fort Crèvecoeur on the Illinois

River, near present-day Peoria. Two years later, he led an expedition down the Mississippi River to its mouth, claiming all the lands through which the river flowed for King Louis XIV of France. He named the land "Louisiana."

La Salle then hoped to create a French empire stretching from the St. Lawrence River to the Gulf of Mexico. In 1684, he sailed from France with a fleet of four ships to establish a colony at the mouth of the Mississippi. He landed by mistake on what is now Matagorda Bay, Texas. Attacked by Indians, La Salle began an overland march in search of the Mississippi. On the way, some of his companions mutinied and killed him.

ALSO READ: EXPLORATION.

LASERS AND MASERS If you want to talk to a friend who is standing a block away, you can shout at each other and try to hear the words. You would hear better if you cupped your hand to your ear. Your hand would "scoop up" the sound waves so that you could hear better. You would be *amplifying* the sound.

Scientists have the same sort of trouble "hearing" the signals sent back by space-rockets. They cannot cup their hands to their ears to "hear" the signals better! But they can amplify the signals. One of the devices they use to do this is called a maser.

"Maser" is a word made up of the first letters of *m*icrowave *a*mplification by *s*timulated *e*mission of *r*adiation. The first maser was built by the U.S. physicist Charles Hard Townes and his team in 1953.

How does a maser work? Substances absorb (take in) and emit (give off) little packages of energy all the time. These little packages of energy are called *photons*. Normally, the energy going into a substance is equal to the energy coming out. In masers, the substance is put into a *high-energy state* (highly excited). In this high-energy state the atoms of a substance will emit energy at a certain rate when triggered by radio waves. The photons that are emitted help make a stronger radio signal. This is called *stimulated emission*.

Masers have been used in the space program to detect and amplify radio signals 100 times weaker than any other kind of amplifier can detect.

Lasers Light is a form of energy, too, and is made up of photons. These photons have higher frequencies than radio signals have, but they behave much the same. If you remember this, and change the "m" in "maser" to "l" for "light", then you will know what the word "laser" means.

Ordinary light—from a lamp or the sun, for example—is made up of many wavelengths. We see these wavelengths as different colors—

▲ *Sieur de La Salle, the French explorer, claims the region of the Mississippi River for France.*

▲ *A thin laser beam can be aimed very accurately at a single point. Laser beams can be used to cut metal.*

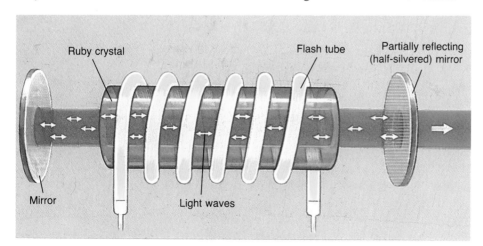

Ruby crystal   Flash tube   Partially reflecting (half-silvered) mirror

Mirror   Light waves

◀ *A ruby laser consists of a flash tube wound around a ruby rod. Tiny pulses of light bounce backward and forward between the two mirrors until a beam of coherent light shoots through the partially reflecting mirror at one end.*

▲ *A powerful laser beam is being used to carry a message to an artificial satellite going around Earth.*

▲ *Lasers are used by doctors to treat some eye complaints. The laser beam can be so fine and so accurately controlled that it may be used to fuse a detached retina (the thin, light-sensitive part of the eye) back into place.*

blue, or red, or yellow. These three colors all together look white. (Other colors are mixtures of these three.) Light from a laser, however, is all exactly the same color; we say it is *monochromatic.*

So what is a laser? One kind of laser has a tube with flat ends. One end is a mirror; the other is a *half-silvered mirror* (it lets out some of the light). The material in the tube may be a ruby, or other suitable substance. Energy (normally light) is pumped into the tube. This energy is absorbed by the atoms of the substance. Because they have an "overload" of energy these atoms become *excited.* They give off photons, but these photons are all of the same wavelength. Many of the photons go off in the wrong direction, but some start zooming back toward the silvered mirror. There they are reflected, and as they shoot through the substance they excite other atoms. Soon there are millions of identical photons zooming backward and forward in the tube. When there are a lot of them, they pass through the half-silvered mirror as a beam of laser light. The photons all travel in the same direction, and the beam does not spread out as an ordinary flashlight beam does. Also, the light waves are *coherent*—they are parallel, with the same peaks and lows. They are exactly the same color (i.e., wavelength).

Scientists have bounced laser beams off the moon and off the planet Venus. By measuring the time taken to travel these huge distances, they were able to tell very accurately how far the moon is from Earth and how big the mountains on Venus are.

In industry, lasers are used as drills. A laser can burn a tiny hole with great accuracy. Doctors find lasers to be useful tools, too. A surgeon using a laser can weld a detached retina back onto an eye. Surgeons may also use a laser to cut away diseased tissue quickly, without harming surrounding healthy tissue.

Lasers are used in holography. Here they are able to help to produce "three-dimensional photographs." They are also being used to improve communications systems, using fiber optics.

ALSO READ: ATOM, COLOR, ENERGY, EYE, FIBER OPTICS, HOLOGRAPHY, LIGHT, MICROWAVES, MIRROR, RADIATION, RADIO, SOUND, WAVE.

LATIN Latin was once one of the most important languages in the world. Today, few people read and write it, and even fewer speak it. And yet, almost everybody in Europe and America uses Latin in his or her speech every day. How can this be?

Latin was the language spoken by the ancient Romans, who lived in Italy. The Romans built up an empire so powerful that its armies were sent to every corner of the known world. In a short time, Latin became the language of trade, schools, churches, and government throughout the Roman Empire. Great works of literature, such as the poems of Virgil and Ovid, were written in Latin. In some areas conquered by the Romans, people almost completely forgot their own languages. The Latin they spoke developed into what are now called the *Romance languages.* Spanish, French, Italian, Portuguese, and Romanian are the major ones.

After the Roman Empire broke up, scholars and clergy throughout Europe continued to speak and write Latin. Many Latin words and forms of grammar became part of the English language. Most European languages used the Latin alphabet. Many Latin words and names are used in biology and zoology and by members of the medical and legal professions. Latin is still used in many mottoes. United States coins, for instance, carry the Latin saying *E Pluribus Unum,* which means "Out of many, one." Latin words are also used as a foundation for forming new words. As an example, in English, every word that starts with "aqua" is using the Latin word for water. A glance at the dictionary shows us such words as aquamarine, aquaplane, aquarium, and aquatic. Latin is studied in many schools throughout the world. Many people believe that mastering the rules of Latin grammar helps you to understand English grammar. Knowing Latin words certainly helps you to understand some English words.

ALSO READ: ALPHABET, ENGLISH LANGUAGE, LANGUAGES, ROMANCE LANGUAGES, ROMAN EMPIRE.

LATIN AMERICA see CENTRAL AMERICA, SOUTH AMERICA.

LATINO see HISPANIC AMERICANS.

LATITUDE AND LONGITUDE

Latitude is a measure of the distance of any point on the Earth's surface north or south of the equator. Longitude is the measure of any point east or west of an imaginary line that runs from the North Pole through Greenwich (a suburb of London, England) to the South Pole.

To measure latitude, the Earth is divided into circles parallel to the equator. Each circle is called a *parallel of latitude*. Latitude is measured in degrees. The equator has a latitude of zero degrees (0°). The North Pole has a latitude of 90° north, and the South Pole a latitude of 90° south. Thus, there are 90 degrees (90°) of latitude between the equator and either of the poles. Each degree is divided into 60 parts, called *minutes*. This is written as: 60′. Each minute is divided into 60 *seconds*. This is written as: 60″. The distance between two parallels of latitude that are one degree apart is about 60 nautical (sea) miles (111

km). A nautical mile is 796 feet (243 m) longer than a land mile.

To measure longitude, the Earth is divided into equally spaced circles running through both the North and South poles. These circles are *meridians of longitude*. Unlike parallels of latitude, meridians are not always at equal distance from each other. The distance between two meridians is widest at the equator and narrows toward the poles, where the meridians meet.

The meridian running through Greenwich is at zero degrees (0°) longitude. Any place halfway around the world from the Greenwich meridian has a longitude of 180°. This meridian divides the Earth into two *hemispheres*, each having 180° of longitude. Any place west of Greenwich has west longitude, and any place east, east

About half of all the English words in use today are of Latin origin. We can hardly speak a sentence without using words such as "city," "army," "religion," "general," "private," "street," and thousands of others that we have inherited from the Romans. We even use whole Latin phrases such as *ad infinitum* or *persona non grata*.

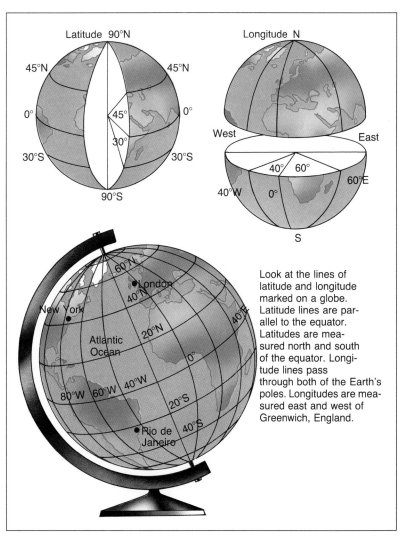

Look at the lines of latitude and longitude marked on a globe. Latitude lines are parallel to the equator. Latitudes are measured north and south of the equator. Longitude lines pass through both of the Earth's poles. Longitudes are measured east and west of Greenwich, England.

Not all the Mormons followed Brigham Young to Utah. Some became members of the Reorganized Church of Jesus Christ of Latter-day Saints, which has its headquarters in Independence, Missouri.

The Mormon Tabernacle Choir is more than a hundred years old. This famous choir gives many concerts, telecasts, and broadcasts. Visitors go to the Tabernacle to hear the choir and the huge pipe organ that dates from 1866.

▼ *The Mormon Tabernacle and office building in Salt Lake City.*

longitude. For example, St. Paul, Minnesota, is at 90° west longitude, and Helsinki, Finland, is at 25° east longitude.

■ LEARN BY DOING

If you know the latitude and longitude of any place, you can locate it on a map or globe of the Earth. Let's say an airplane pilot radios this message: "I am at 22° north latitude and 157° west longitude." Find on a map the point where that parallel and meridian cross. ■

ALSO READ: EARTH, EQUATOR, GEOGRAPHY, INTERNATIONAL DATE LINE, MAP.

LATTER-DAY SAINTS The people who belong to the Church of Jesus Christ of Latter-day Saints are usually called *Mormons*. Joseph Smith founded the church in 1830. Smith claimed he had a revelation, or vision, in which God told him to start a new faith. In another vision, Smith said, an angel showed him where to find a set of golden plates, or tablets, with Egyptian writing on them. Smith said he translated these writings. His translation has come to be known as *The Book of Mormon—Another Testament of Jesus Christ*. Mormons consider the writings to be holy scripture along with the Bible.

The new religion grew, and Smith moved his followers to Kirtland, Ohio. Many people in Kirtland did not want the Mormons to live there, and forced them to move away. They went to Missouri and then to Illinois, where they founded the city of Nauvoo. After a few years there, Joseph Smith was killed by an angry mob. Brigham Young became the new leader, and the Mormons moved once again, this time to the Great Salt Lake valley in Utah. Today, there are more than six million members of the church world wide; about one million live in Utah.

ALSO READ: SMITH, JOSEPH; UTAH; YOUNG, BRIGHAM.

LATVIA Latvia, a land of rolling hills and fertile soil, is one of the three Soviet republics on the Baltic Sea. The other two are Estonia to the north and Lithuania to the south. Two Russian republics of the Soviet Union are eastern neighbors. (See the map with the article on EUROPE.) To the west, Latvia has almost 300 miles (483 km) of coast along the Baltic Sea and the Gulf of Riga. This gulf freezes over in winter. In summer, the weather is mild in Latvia. Riga, a Baltic port city, is the capital and largest city of the country.

The Latvians, also known as Letts, are an ancient people with a rich culture. They have lived along the Gulf of Riga for almost 2,000 years. Their language, Lettish, is one of the oldest now spoken in Europe. Their land has been under foreign rule many times. From the middle 1200's to the middle 1500's, the Latvians had to work the land for German knights and nobles. The Poles gained control of Latvia in the 1500's, and the Swedes ruled northern Latvia during the 1600's. Russia began to dominate the country in the 1700's and ruled until Latvia won independence in 1918. The Latvians divided

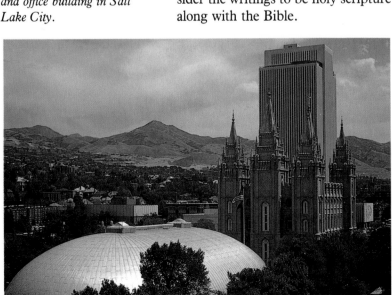

the land among the peasants and elected a democratic government. But the Russians conquered them again in 1940. The Germans occupied Latvia during World War II from 1941 to 1944. The Soviet Union again took control of the land and named it the Latvian Soviet Socialist Republic.

The country has many cattle dairy farms. Other farms breed sheep, hogs, poultry, and horses. The main crops are potatoes, barley, oats, and rye. Latvian factories produce textiles, machinery, motors, electronic equipment, ships, and processed foods.

The United States and a few other countries do not recognize the Soviet Union's control of Latvia. They regard Latvia as an independent nation.

ALSO READ: BALTIC SEA, ESTONIA, LITHUANIA, RUSSIAN HISTORY.

LAUNDRIES AND DRY CLEANERS

No one knows where or when the very first laundry began. Perhaps it began 2,000 years ago in ancient Rome, where people were paid to wash clothes.

In 1849 and 1850, the thousands of prospectors who rushed to California to dig for gold had to launder their own clothes. One day a man named Davis decided to open a laundry to earn money for food. He started the Contra Costa Laundry in 1851 in Oakland, California. After a while, he put in a washing machine operated by a steam engine. Soon his laundry was more valuable than some gold mines.

Today, thousands of commercial laundries have big, automatic washing machines and dryers. Many cities have self-service "laundromats," where people do their laundry in coin-operated machines.

In commercial laundries, the things to be washed are sorted according to colors and fabrics. Bed linens, towels, and other strong fabrics or white things are washed in water hot

enough to scald your hands. Darker colors are washed at lower temperatures, and *synthetic* (man-made) fabrics are usually washed at medium-warm temperatures. The wash that belongs to one family is put into numbered net bags to keep the clothes all together while they are in the washing machine. Before clothes are dried, the wash is put into *extractors* or *spinners*. Extractors are large tubs with holes in the sides. They spin the clothes around at very high speeds to remove most of the water from the wash. Then some of the clothes are ironed while they are still damp. Other clothes are dried in machines (*tumble driers*) that tumble them around, while air—at any temperature from room temperature to very hot—is blown through them.

Some materials, such as linen, silk, and wool, may shrink or fade if washed in soap and water. So these fabrics are often *dry cleaned* instead of laundered. Dry cleaning is done with special kinds of chemicals. *Solvents* used in dry cleaning dissolve and remove grease and dirt. The process is called "dry" cleaning, because no water is used.

Some kind of dry cleaning was used several thousand years ago in Greece and Rome. Persons called *fullers* made cloth and yarn thicker by wetting and pressing it, but first they

▲ *Modern dry-cleaning methods rely on chemicals to remove the dirt and grease from the clothes.*

▲ *In poor countries where there is no supply of running water in the home, people have to go down to the stream or river to do their laundry.*

1397

▲ *Sir Wilfrid Laurier, the great Canadian statesman.*

cleaned the cloth and yarn with *fuller's earth*, a kind of soft clay that removes grease spots. It was probably the first substance used for dry cleaning. Modern dry cleaning was invented in Paris in 1849 by a French tailor, Jolly Belin. In those days, dry cleaning was done by hand. Now it is done by automatic machinery.

ALSO READ: SOAPS AND DETERGENTS.

LAURIER, SIR WILFRID (1841–1919) Sir Wilfrid Laurier, a Canadian statesman, became the first French-Canadian prime minister of Canada. He was born in St. Lin, Quebec, just north of Montreal. Laurier's family spoke only French, so they sent him to live for two years with an English-speaking family, and to attend an English school. He graduated from both a French college and an English university. Therefore, he understood both the English-speaking and the French-speaking peoples.

Laurier found the influence of the church in Quebec too old-fashioned. He joined a political party that was working to modernize French Canada. Later, he joined the Liberal Party in the Canadian federal government and was soon chosen to be the party's leader. He was elected prime minister in 1896. As prime minister, he worked to bring about cooperation between the French-speaking and English-speaking groups of Canada. He encouraged people to settle in western Canada, and had miles of railroad tracks and roads built.

Laurier also worked hard to make trade easier between Canada and other countries. His government was finally defeated in 1911. He was voted out of office when he tried to persuade Canadians to make an agreement with the United States that neither country would tax imported goods from the other.

ALSO READ: CANADA.

▲ *Antoine Lavoisier, the French chemist. Among his many achievements was the discovery that air is a mixture of gases. He was guillotined during the French Revolution.*

LAVA see VOLCANO.

LAVOISIER, ANTOINE LAURENT (1743–1794) Antoine Lavoisier, a French scientist, was a founder of modern chemistry. He was the first to explain what burning is—the rapid combining of a material with oxygen. He also explained that breathing is a kind of slow burning process. In a famous series of experiments, he proved that in chemical changes, such as burning, matter is neither created nor destroyed. It is only changed in form.

Lavoisier made his discoveries mainly by extending and improving the work of other scientists, and then proving his new ideas by brilliant experiments. He was one of the first to use careful measurement as a tool.

Lavoisier was born in Paris, France, to a wealthy family. In school, he showed great interest in science. His wealth made it possible for him to spend most of his life in scientific work. His most important discovery was that air is a mixture of two gases (we now know there are small quantities of others). He called these two gases "oxygen" and "nitrogen."

Lavoisier was a member of a group that collected taxes for King Louis XVI. In 1789, the French Revolution broke out, and the king was dethroned. Lavoisier was executed, along with the other members of the group, in 1794.

ALSO READ: CHEMISTRY; ELEMENT; FRENCH REVOLUTION; LOUIS, KINGS OF FRANCE; RESPIRATION.

LAW Small children are told they must not cross the street by themselves. Teenagers may be told not to play music so loudly that they disturb other family members. Parents set up rules, or laws, to protect children and to make it easier for members of a household to live together.

Law is a set of rules that regulates the actions of each member of a group of people, for the good of the entire group. The group may be as small as a family or as large as a nation, but it must have some kind of law to help people to get along with each other. Law, whether written or unwritten, is based on people's past experiences in living. A very old set of laws is the Ten Commandments. These are laws of proper behavior that persons followed thousands of years ago and still follow today. Law should be a "living" thing. This means that, as social habits and customs change, the law should be *flexible*, or able to change with them. Two basic systems of law used in the world today are the English common-law system and the Napoleonic Code.

English Common Law English common law began about 1,000 years ago. Under the Saxons (early tribesmen who lived in England), laws were called "dooms" (sometimes spelled "domes") or "ordinances." People with complaints would go before the local lord who would decide what should be done. After the Normans from northern France conquered the Anglo-Saxons in 1066, local decisions were handled by "king's courts." The king sent his royal judges to all parts of the kingdom to listen to arguments and make decisions in his name. These decisions became *precedents* (examples to be followed).

The early colonists brought their knowledge of English common law to the New World. U.S. law is based on the English common law. Law students today study common law based on the study of precedents.

There are many "branches" of common law. *Civil law* deals with decisions that affect people's daily life. It handles such things as accidents, damages, contracts, and property arguments. If somebody owes

you money and refuses to pay it back, you may take the case to a civil-law court.

Whenever a society has law, it also has ways of dealing with lawbreakers. *Criminal law* handles acts such as burglary, kidnapping, and murder, which harm individuals or the community. Penalties for criminal acts are also based on precedents. The lawbreaker is punished in the name of the rest of society.

Laws made by kings or legislative bodies, such as parliaments or congresses, are called *statute law*. Statute law can explain things that are unclear in civil law, and can overrule (change) the decisions made in civil-law courts.

The Napoleonic Code So many different laws existed in France in the 1700's that the philosopher Voltaire said, "A traveler in France has to change laws as frequently as he changes horses." In 1804, Napoleon I appointed a group of judges to figure out a system of law for all of France. They wrote down a detailed system of law, which came to be called the Napoleonic Code. It was a combination of Germanic law and Roman law. A version of the Napoleonic Code is

▲ *This stone block was discovered early this century. Inscribed on it is the Code of Hammurabi, a king of Babylon during the 18th century B.C. The code is one of the oldest known systems of laws.*

▼ *A Dutch law court of the early 18th century.*

▲ *International law is seen here being put into action. The occasion is the signing of the Rhodesian ceasefire agreement in December 1979.*

In the United States there is one lawyer for every 400 citizens. In Britain there is one for every 1,400 persons, and in Japan, a lawyer for every 10,000 persons.

still used in France. Many other nations also use the Code as a model for their own legal systems. Part of the legal system of the state of Louisiana is based on it.

Other Forms of Law   *Constitutional law* deals with the rights and powers of persons and governments under rules set down in their constitutions. The job of the Supreme Court is to explain the laws contained in the Constitution. The court can rule that some decision or law is *unconstitutional* (against the Constitution). It can also overrule the findings of a lower court. State supreme courts explain the laws contained in state constitutions.

Military law applies to any person in the army, navy, or other branch of the military. The U.S. military has its own courts and system of punishment. In 1951, Congress passed laws changing some of the military codes. Congress decided that the same code should be used for all branches of military service. This was done to make sure that enlisted persons (those who are not officers) get fair treatment, and to allow civilian (nonmilitary) lawyers to appear at military trials.

International law applies to conduct between nations. International law is difficult to apply or enforce, because

it is not backed by one nation or legal system. If a country or group of countries "break" an international law, there is really no way to punish them. The United Nations is working on a solution to this problem.

For further information on:
Careers in Law, *see* FEDERAL BUREAU OF INVESTIGATION; HOLMES FAMILY; LAWYERS AND JUDGES; MARSHALL, JOHN; MARSHALL, THURGOOD.
History of Law, *see* CONSTITUTION, UNITED STATES; ENGLISH HISTORY; FRENCH HISTORY; GERMAN HISTORY; MAGNA CARTA.
Kinds of Law, *see* CHILD LABOR, CIVIL RIGHTS, INTERNATIONAL LAW, LEAGUE OF NATIONS, MARRIAGE, PASSPORTS AND VISAS, PATENTS AND COPYRIGHTS, PROHIBITION, STATES' RIGHTS, TREATY, UNITED NATIONS.
Legal Systems, *see* CRIME; CONGRESS, UNITED STATES; COURT SYSTEM; JUVENILE DELINQUENCY; LEGISLATURE; PARLIAMENT, SUPREME COURT; TRIAL.

LAWN BOWLS   see BOWLING.

LAWRENCE OF ARABIA (1888–1935) Thomas Edward Lawrence was an archeologist, writer, and soldier. He was the author of a famous book about the Middle East called *The Seven Pillars of Wisdom* (1926). It tells about his adventures in the Arab world. He wrote several other popular books, including *Crusader Castles* (1936). As "Lawrence of Arabia," he is remembered as a romantic adventurer and soldier. Lawrence was born in Wales and later educated at Oxford University.

During World War I, Lawrence joined the British Intelligence Service in Egypt. At that time, the British were encouraging the Arab subjects of the Ottoman Empire to revolt against their Turkish rulers. As a British officer, Lawrence organized and led the Arab armies.

After the war, Lawrence felt that Britain had been unfair to the Arabs by helping the Jews make Palestine a Jewish state, taking it away from the Arabs. He resigned from his job in the British Colonial Office in 1922 and enlisted as a private in the Royal Air Force.

Lawrence did not enjoy being treated like a famous person. To escape the publicity attached to his name, he changed it first to J. H. Ross and then to T. E. Shaw. He died in a motorcycle accident in England.

ALSO READ: MIDDLE EAST, OTTOMAN EMPIRE.

LAWYERS AND JUDGES People living in a simple society did not need lawyers. In frontier days, for example, few lawyers were needed in the little settlements of the West. A circuit judge (a traveling judge who covered an area) would ride into town now and then to hear the few cases that had arisen. In modern times, however, the laws are so many and so complicated that the ordinary person cannot possibly know them all. When someone has a special need to know about certain laws, he or she must get the services of a lawyer, also called an *attorney*, a *counselor*, or a *solicitor*.

A lawyer is the legal representative of persons, or groups, or governments, in their disputes or relations with each other. He or she may represent a government (and its citizens), or a business. Some lawyers deal only with cases of a certain kind, such as corporate law (business affairs), divorce law (law dealing with marriage dissolvements), real estate law (law dealing with buying and selling property), maritime law (law dealing with ships), or criminal law (law dealing with people accused of committing crimes). Lawyers spend much of their time advising their *clients* (customers) about what they legally can or cannot do. In this way, lawyers often keep people out of trouble.

A lawyer may be *retained*, or hired, for many reasons. A lawyer may draw up a *contract* (agreement) between a person who has something to sell and a person who wants to buy it. There are many state and federal laws about handling the *estate* (money and property) of someone who has died. A person who wants his or her money and property handled in a certain way will get a lawyer to draw up a *will*. The will states exactly what will be done with the person's estate after that person dies.

In any criminal trial in the United States, the *defendant* (accused person) has the right to be represented by a lawyer. If the defendant cannot afford to pay a lawyer, the court will appoint one and pay the fee. Lawyers are required to use all their knowledge of the law to help their client. Even if persons are guilty, they have the right to have their cases presented in the best possible way.

To become a lawyer, persons must study the laws of their state and country. They must learn about past legal cases and decisions. They attend law school for three years after they have graduated from college. They must then pass a *bar* (law) examination in the state where they want to work and be interviewed by a committee of lawyers. If they pass the examination and are considered to be of good

▲ *T.E. Lawrence, the British soldier and writer known as Lawrence of Arabia.*

▼ *British law maintains some ancient customs. Here, High Court judges are in procession with their clerks. The judges wear full-dress robes, hoods and mantles.*

character, they are sworn in before a judge. They can then practice law in that state. If a lawyer breaks any rules of conduct set by a state legislature, he or she may be *disbarred* (prevented from practicing law).

In the United States, most people who become judges are lawyers. A judge presides over a trial in a court of law. He or she may explain legal points, instruct the jury, and pass a sentence after the jury has delivered the *verdict* (decision). Judges are either appointed by the governor or elected. This usually depends on the state law or the kind of court the judge will preside over. Members of the Supreme Court are appointed by the President, but must be approved by the Senate.

ALSO READ: COURT SYSTEM, LAW, SUPREME COURT, TRIAL.

LEAF A leaf is a flat or slightly curved green structure that grows from the stem of a plant. Leaves do not grow on every kind of plant. Simple plants, such as algae, do not have leaves. Mosses and some other plants have structures that look much like leaves, but under a microscope, differences can be seen.

Shapes and Parts of Leaves

Leaves have an amazing variety of shapes. Oak and pine trees, rosebushes, corn plants, and grass all have leaves—as do thousands of other kinds of plants—and all these leaves have different shapes. In fact, if you were to study carefully every single leaf on one large tree, you would discover that no two of them are exactly alike!

Some leaves are round and some are long and thin. Some leaves have smooth edges, but others have edges that look like saw teeth. Evergreen leaves look like needles or tiny lances.

Leaves of maple, oak, elm, and fruit trees are called *simple leaves.* They are all in one part. The leaves of clover, rosebushes, and walnut and butternut trees are *compound leaves.* Each of these leaves is made up of several *leaflets* (little leaves).

The broad, flat part of a leaf is the *blade.* Many kinds of leaves are attached to the plant stem by a thin stalk. This stalk is the *petiole.* If you look closely at the undersides of most leaves, you will see *veins*, a network of tiny tubes that carry water, food, and minerals into and out of the leaf. The veins also act as a kind of skeleton, keeping the leaf from collapsing.

A Tiny Food Factory The most amazing feature of leaves is that each one is a tiny "food factory." Only green plants—those that contain the substance *chlorophyll*—can make their own food.

A leaf uses two raw materials—water and a gas present in the air called *carbon dioxide*—to make food. It gets energy from sunlight to combine these two materials. A leaf combines the water and carbon dioxide to make its "food," *glucose,* which is a kind of sugar. The leaf then changes the glucose to starch. The chlorophyll helps the leaf combine the water and carbon dioxide by absorbing energy in the form of sunlight. The process of making starch is called *photosynthe-*

▼ *Leaves are green because they contain a substance called* chlorophyll. *In the fall, however, many leaves become red, orange, yellow, or brown because chlorophyll is no longer present. The fall coloration occurs because the colors of other substances in the leaves, called* carotenes, *can now be seen.*

Black walnut

Red maple
(Palmate veins)

American elm
(Pinnate veins)

Beech

White birch

Blade

Midrib

Large vein

Horse chestnut
(Palmate
compound)

White oak

Petiole

Basswood

Tulip

Sycamore

Red oak

White ash
(Pinnate compound)

White pine

Balsam fir
(Needlelike)

Some leaves have special jobs. The *tendrils* of peas and melons look like tiny wire coils. They hold the plants up by gripping a pole or fence. Cactus *spines* are sharp needles that guard the plant and prevent water loss.

▲ *After the slaughter of World War I, many nations sought a lasting peace. The League of Nations was set up in 1920 with the aim of settling quarrels peacefully. It lasted for 26 years.*

sis, which comes from Greek words that mean "to put together with light." All life depends on the process—because otherwise the *food web* would not work.

An Important Part of Life One result of photosynthesis is that oxygen is produced when the leaf takes in carbon dioxide from the air. All other living things stay alive only because of this. Plants are the first step in the food web. For example, cattle and sheep eat plants. Other animals—including people—eat the cattle and sheep. People also eat leaves, such as the leaves of lettuce and cabbage plants. Can you think of some other leaves people eat?

Leaves are important for other reasons, too. Some leaves, such as mint, flavor your food. Tea is made from the leaves of the tea plant. Drugs are made from the leaves of many kinds of plants. Many dyes, such as indigo (dark blue), are also made from leaves. In some tropical areas, large leaves are even used to construct the ceilings and walls of houses.

■ LEARN BY DOING

You can easily study the process of photosynthesis. Ask your parents to get some iodine and some alcohol from the druggist for you. Pin strips of tinfoil or black paper across the upper sides of one or two leaves on a living plant. Do not cover the whole leaf. Leave the plant in a sunny place for two or three days. At the end of a sunny day, cut the partly covered leaves from the plant. Remove the covering strips, and soak the leaves in alcohol overnight.

Take the leaves out of the alcohol. Using a medicine dropper, put drops of iodine all over the tops of each leaf. Iodine turns blue when starch is present. What does your test show? ■

ALSO READ: CHEMISTRY, CONIFER, DRUG, FOOD WEB, PHOTOSYNTHESIS, PLANT, PLANT KINGDOM, TREE.

LEAGUE OF NATIONS At the end of World War I, the victorious nations, including the United Kingdom, France, Italy, and the United States, decided that there must never be another war. They felt that the way to prevent war was to form an organization of nations that would work for world peace and international cooperation. This organization, the League of Nations, was established in 1920, with its headquarters at Geneva, Switzerland. Forty-seven nations were members at the beginning, and several others joined later.

The member nations of the League agreed to bring their disagreements to the League Council for advice, instead of immediately going to war. The League set up agencies to help nations improve the health, education, trade, industry, and transportation of their countries.

Woodrow Wilson, who was President of the United States at the time, was one of the main organizers of the League. The United States never joined the League, because the Senate refused to approve the League's constitution. Without the United States as a member, the League was weakened from the start. It was further weakened when Japan and Germany withdrew in 1933. Italy, the Soviet Union, and others dropped out of the League later.

In its short life, the League of Nations settled a number of small disputes and helped improve conditions in many countries. But it failed to stop Japan's invasion of Manchuria (part of China) in 1931 and Italy's attack on Ethiopia in 1935. It also failed to prevent World War II. The League was ended after the war in 1946, but it served as a model for the United Nations, which replaced it.

ALSO READ: INTERNATIONAL RELATIONS; WILSON, WOODROW; UNITED NATIONS.

LEAKEY FAMILY One Kenyan family has discovered much of what we know about our earliest ancestors. They are Louis Seymour Bazett (L.S.B.) Leakey (1903–1972), his wife Mary (born 1913), and their sons, most notably Richard Erskine Frere Leakey (born 1944). They have proved that humans existed in the world much earlier than anyone had thought. Also, they have shown that human beings first appeared in Africa, not Asia, as people had believed.

The first major discovery was made by Mary in 1959 in Olduvai Gorge, Tanzania. It was a fossil of a hominid (any of a family of bipedal primate mammals) thought to be 1,750,000 years old. It was named *Zinjanthropus*. It is now believed to be a type of *Australopithecus* (a very early hominid). But L.S.B. concluded that a hominid called *Homo habilis*, which lived about the same time, was our true ancestor.

The Leakeys kept finding older fossil hominids. In 1972, Richard found a fossil skull (Skull 1470), believed to be about 2,000,000 years old. In 1974, Mary found remains thought to be as much as 3,750,000 years old.

Richard did exciting work in the 1960's and 1970's at a place called Koobi Fora, by Lake Turkana, Kenya. Here he and his team found not only Skull 1470, which is almost complete, but also about 400 other human fossil remains.

ALSO READ: ANTHROPOLOGY, ARCHEOLOGY, FOSSIL, HUMAN BEINGS.

LEANING TOWER OF PISA
Most buildings that look as if they are falling over soon do, but the famous Leaning Tower of Pisa in Italy has been leaning for more than 600 years! The tower is the *campanile* (bell tower) of the cathedral in Pisa.

Builders began work on the bell tower in 1173. The stone foundation they built was not strong enough to support the heavy tower, and it began to sink unevenly in the soft soil. The tower was already leaning when it was finished in 1372. It now leans 17 feet (5.18 m) to one side, and the tilt increases by about .0393 inches (1 mm) each year. Some architects say the tower will fall down within the next 100 years. In 1987 the Italian government approved a plan to reinforce the tower's foundation and keep the landmark from toppling.

The round tower is made of white marble and is 182 feet (55.5 m) high. Six of its eight stories are surrounded by a series of arches supported by 30 columns. If you have enough energy to climb almost 300 steps on a circular stairway, you can look out from the top and see the entire city of Pisa.

LEAP YEAR see TIME.

LEAR, EDWARD (1812–1888)
The British writer Edward Lear described himself in one of his own poems.

"How pleasant to know Mr. Lear!
Who has written such volumes of stuff!
Some think him ill-tempered and queer,
But a few think him pleasant enough."

Lear was born in London, England. He became a commercial artist at age 15. Painting with watercolors was his specialty. He worked for the London Zoological Society, making highly accurate, beautiful paintings of birds, particularly parrots. Lear's bird pictures won him a job with the Earl of Derby, sketching the animals in the earl's private zoo. Lear often entertained the earl's grandchildren with his comic poems and drawings. His delightful first *Book of Nonsense* (1846) was dedicated to them. More nonsense books were published later.

▲ *The Leaning Tower of Pisa, Italy, was begun in 1173 and completed in 1372. The tilt is becoming greater. Unless this great landmark is repaired, it will fall to the ground.*

▲ *Dr. Louis Seymour Bazett Leakey, the celebrated Kenyan anthropologist.*

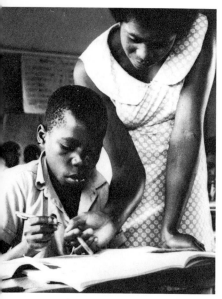

▲ *Learning at a school in Lusaka, Zambia.*

One of his most famous nonsense poems is about "The Owl and the Pussycat," who went to sea
"In a beautiful pea-green boat;
They took some honey, and plenty of money
Wrapped up in a five-pound note."
Other strange characters in Lear's nonsense books are "The Pobble Who Has no Toes," who swam across the Bristol Channel, and "The Dong with the Luminous Nose." The Dong wanders about
"When awful darkness and silence reign
Over the great Gromboolian plain."

Lear traveled a great deal, visiting Italy, Greece, Albania, and the Near East. He painted scenes and landscapes with watercolors wherever he went, and published several illustrated travel books. His travel books are good, but his nonsense verses made him more famous. He also wrote many amusing five-line poems called *limericks*, and soon people all over the country were reciting his limericks and making up their own. This is one of his:
"There was an old man with a beard,
Who said, 'It is just as I feared!
Two Owls and a Hen,
Four Larks and a Wren,
Have all built their nests in my beard.' "

ALSO READ: LIMERICK, PAINTING.

LEARNING Do you remember the first time you tried to roller-skate or ride a bicycle? You are probably able to skate or ride much better now than you could then! This skill is the result of the process of learning. When you look up something in this encyclopedia, you are usually interested in learning something. Many other people have already learned what is written here, and because you have already learned to read, you can share their knowledge.

What is learning? Scientists have

tried for many years to answer this question. One answer is that learning is a process by which people use their past experiences to determine their behavior, classify information, and form habits.

Learning takes place every day of your life from the time you are born. As a baby, you discovered that if you cried when you were hungry you would be fed. You also learned to cry when you were uncomfortable or lonely. You learned from past experiences that if you cried your parents would feed or comfort you.

Learning How to Learn The most important learning is "learning how to learn." We talk about "learning" the multiplication tables or "learning" the correct spelling of words. These are learned *facts*. But only the person who knows *how* to learn can take these facts or information and question them, connect them to what he

▼ *Learning languages can be as much fun as a video game. A good program asks you to compete against the computer.*

▲ *Microcomputers can process data, handle words, and carry out calculations. They can be used as a personal teaching aid also.*

or she already knows, and reach conclusions.

"Connecting" information is an important part of learning. Often scientists make discoveries because they connect one piece of information with another. For example, the great British scientist Isaac Newton is said to have seen an apple fall from a tree, looked at the moon orbiting (going around) the Earth, and realized that there was a connection between the two things. Because he had *connected* the two bits of information in his mind, he was able to learn about gravity.

You have probably discovered this yourself. Remember when you learned to throw a baseball. You learned how to stand, balance yourself, swing your arm, and aim the ball. Now you do not have too much trouble throwing another type of ball—e.g., a basketball. The balance, swing, and timing are different, but you have learned all the basic principles. Learning to play one ball game helps you play all the others.

How Does Learning Take Place?
There are no easy ways to explain just how people learn. It is known, however, that learning must be stimulated. A *stimulus* is a kind of signal that alerts one or more of the senses (sight, hearing, touch, taste, and smell). A person then *reacts* or *responds* to the stimulus. Most often, this response is some kind of movement. For instance, you hear a door open (stimulus), and you look up (response) to see who is entering the room. Or you hear a baby in a crib cry (stimulus), and you go (response) to find out why he or she is crying. In both cases, you respond because of past learning. You look up to see who is entering the room because from past experience you know that the sound of a door being opened means that someone is coming. You go to check on the baby because from past experience you know that the crying means that he or she needs or wants something.

Reasons and Rewards People who study the nature of learning are called *educational psychologists*. They work with animals, children, and adults as the "subjects" of their studies. Although psychologists have developed many different ideas about learning, most of them agree that people learn faster if they have some *motivation* (a real need or desire) to learn. You learn your lines if you want to do well in a class play. Sometimes the satisfaction you feel as a result of learning is a kind of motivation. A high grade or higher pay is another kind of motivation. For the student, the reward is often the knowledge that he or she has learned a subject well.

We learn things more easily during the first 15 to 20 years of life. In our late teens our brain is as mature as it will ever be. Then there is a period of about 20 years during which learning ability stays about the same. After this period it becomes increasingly difficult to learn new things and our memory deteriorates.

▼ *A first step in learning how to swim is to practice with a kickboard. Wanting to learn a new skill is very important in all forms of learning.*

Leather from the hides of cattle can be up to a third of an inch (10 mm) thick. This thickness of leather can be used for the soles of shoes, but usually it is split into two or three thinner layers. The top layer will have the leather "grain," and the other layers are used to make "suede" leather.

Methods of Learning Learning and teaching are so closely connected that any article about learning must also mention teaching methods. Laboratory schools try out different teaching methods, or ways of teaching, in order to find the best ways to bring about learning.

Another teaching method is *programmed learning*. This uses a teaching machine that provides a stimulus (question) to the learner who then makes a response (answer). If the answer is correct, another question is given. If the answer is wrong, the information is taught again, and the question is repeated. In this way, if the student does not learn the first time, he or she has another chance. The machine also leads the learner through a series of steps, each one more advanced than the one before, until he or she acquires the skill or knowledge being taught.

ALSO READ: EDUCATION, INTELLIGENCE, MEMORY, SCHOOL.

LEATHER The very useful material called leather is made from the skins of animals. Most of these skins come from animals bred to provide food for people (e.g., cows, sheep, goats, pigs). The skin is considered to be a secondary product of the meatpacking industry. But many wild animals, such as alligators, kangaroos, and lizards, are often killed just to supply skins to make leather. For this reason, some wild animals are in danger of being killed off entirely (becoming extinct). Many people refuse to buy products made from the skins of these animals.

Early people probably made their first articles of clothing from animal skins with fur and hair still on them. Since then, people have found ways to treat animal skins to shape them into shoes, gloves, suitcases, bookbindings, furniture covering, footballs, and many other products.

The process by which an animal skin is treated is called *tanning* and takes place in factories called *tanneries*. Each skin may be treated by various tanning processes, depending on the use for which the leather is intended. The two main tanning processes are *vegetable tanning* and *mineral*, or *chrome*, *tanning*.

Before tanning, the raw skins are "cured" by being soaked in *brine* (salt water) for a few weeks. Next, the skins are soaked in pure water to remove all salt, dirt, and blood. The flesh and hair on the skins are removed by chemicals (lime and sodium sulfide) and machines. The skins are then soaked in a weak solution of acid to reduce the swelling caused by the lime. At the same time, the skins are treated with an enzyme solution to make the skin soft and flexible. Then the skins are ready to be tanned.

In vegetable tanning, the skins are treated with a strong solution of *tannin*, a chemical made from tree bark. This makes the leather very strong and water-resistant. *Flexible* (able to stretch or bend) vegetable-tanned leathers to be used for luggage or upholstery are less heavily tanned than leather for shoe soles.

In mineral, or chrome, tanning, the skins are treated with a solution of various chemicals, usually containing chromium. Chrome-tanned leathers stretch more than vegetable-tanned leathers and can be used for handbags, shoes, gloves, and clothing. Sometimes skins are chrome-tanned and then vegetable-tanned, to pro-

▼ *These hides have been tanned (treated so that they will not rot) and are now hanging out to dry in the sunshine.*

duce a leather having the advantages of each type.

Tanned leather is stiff, and must be oiled to soften it. Then the leather is dyed, cut, and shaped into the final product. Leather for various purposes will receive many different kinds of treatment. For example, several coats of a thick, oily varnish are needed to give *patent leather* its high gloss. Leather is still in use, but modern factories now make synthetic (man-made) materials that look and feel like leather, but artificial leathers are less expensive than leather and are much easier to care for.

ALSO READ: MANUFACTURING, PLASTIC, SHOES.

LEBANON Beautiful Mediterranean beaches and snow-capped mountains, the ruins of ancient cities, and castles built by the Crusaders are features of Lebanon that once attracted tourists. The tourism industry has collapsed, however, because of civil war and other conflict.

Lebanon's capital, Beirut, is a leading communications and transportation center. (See the map with the article on the MIDDLE EAST.) Lebanon has four geographical regions. A narrow coastal plain in the west joins the Lebanon Mountains. East of this mountain range is the narrow, fertile valley of Al Biqa. Another mountain range called the Anti-Lebanon rises

on the eastern side of the valley, and continues into Syria. Lebanon has basically only two seasons. Winters are cool and moist, and summers are warm and dry.

Over two-fifths of the Lebanese earn their living in agriculture. Wheat and barley are the main crops, and livestock raising is also important. Fruits are grown along the coastal plain. Trade, however, is a more important part of the Lebanese economy than agriculture. The country trades with other nations of the Middle East and with the rest of the world. Pipelines bring oil from Saudi Arabia and Iraq. The oil is loaded into tankers and shipped to other nations. The Lebanese also earn money from banking, oil-refining, food-processing, and textile-manufacturing.

In most Middle Eastern countries (except Israel) the majority of the

▲ *The sunny Mediterranean beaches of Lebanon are in sharp contrast to the war-torn streets of its capital, Beirut.*

LEBANON

Capital City: Beirut (1,500,000 people).
Area: 4,015 square miles (10,400 sq. km).
Population: 2,800,000.
Government: Republic.
Natural Resources: Iron ore.
Export Products: Jewelry, precious metals and stones, textiles.
Units of Money: Lebanese pound.
Official Language: Arabic.

people are Muslims. In Lebanon, however, about half of the people are Christians and half are Muslims.

Ancient Lebanon was a part of the Phoenician Empire, and later a part of the Byzantine Empire. In those days, it was noted for the fine cedarwood that came from its forests. In the A.D. 800's it came under Arab control. French Crusaders occupied the land between the 1000's and 1300's. The Turks ruled the land from 1516 to 1918. Then the French took over and governed until 1943, when Lebanon became an independent republic. Guerrilla warfare has been waged between Lebanese "Christians" and "Muslims" and between Palestinian commandos and Israeli forces in southern Lebanon.

ALSO READ: BYZANTINE EMPIRE, MIDDLE EAST, PHOENICIA.

▲ *Robert E. Lee, commander in chief of the Confederate armies.*

LEE, ROBERT E. (1807–1870) January 19 is a day of celebration in some Southern states. It is the birthday of Robert E. Lee, commander in chief of the Confederate Army during the Civil War. He was a highly respected military leader, admired not only by his own soldiers, but by Northerners as well.

Robert Edward Lee was born in Stratford, Virginia. His father, Henry "Light Horse Harry" Lee, had been a brilliant general in the American Revolution. As a young man, Robert E. Lee attended the U.S. Military Academy at West Point, and graduated with honors.

He served in Georgia, Virginia, Ohio, and New York in his early army career. While in Virginia, he married Mary Custis, great-granddaughter of George Washington's wife, Martha. The Lees had seven children and lived in the Custis mansion in Arlington, Virginia, on a hill overlooking Washington, D.C.

Lee fought for the first time in 1846, when the Mexican War broke out. He became famous for his skill and courage, and was promoted to *brevet* (honorary) colonel. In 1852, he became superintendent of the U.S. Military Academy at West Point for three years. Then he was assigned to duty on the Texas frontier. When Texas dropped out of the Union in 1861, Lee was sent back to Washington, D.C. and President Abraham Lincoln offered him the field command of the U.S. Army in the war against the South.

Lee had to make a difficult decision. He was not in favor of slavery, and he was not in favor of a divided nation. But he had a great love for the South and for his home state, Virginia. He felt that individual freedom—freedom for every person to live as they please—was the main issue in the South's position, and he was in favor of that. He decided to join the Confederate Army, and he hoped the war would not last long. At first he served as a military adviser to Jefferson Davis. He was promoted to full general in May 1861. One year later, after serving in South Carolina and western Virginia, he took command of the Confederate Army of Northern Virginia. Lee scored some important military victories in Virginia, but he lost important battles at Antietam, Maryland, and Gettysburg, Pennsylvania.

Lee was made commander in chief of all the Confederate armies in February 1865. At that time, the Confederate forces were already in retreat. Lee knew that he was losing. On April 9, 1865, he surrendered to General Ulysses S. Grant, commander in chief of the Union forces, at the Appomattox Court House in Virginia.

Lee became president of Washington College in Lexington, Virginia, after the war. He quickly improved the college and started new programs, including schools of commerce and journalism. After his death, the college was renamed Washington and Lee University.

LEGEND The word "legend" instantly brings colorful pictures to mind. The adventures of King Arthur and Robin Hood and the tales told about Davy Crockett are legends. People have always loved to listen to marvelous stories. Through the years, countless storytellers have spun wonderful tales to fascinate their listeners. Some of the old folk tales were called *myths*, and were about gods and goddesses, and imaginary happenings. A legend is a story that is told as true, but cannot be proved. It may have some truth to it, and it may be about a real person or a real place. But it is usually an exaggeration of what really happened. Many folk tales were passed on by word of mouth. But legends were usually written down. The word "legend" comes from a Latin word, *legenda*, meaning "things to be read."

Legends of Long Ago Legends were carried all over the ancient world by travelers, merchants, sailors, and wandering tribes. Some of the earliest recorded legends were told in the cold, icy land of the Vikings, where storytellers made the long winters seem shorter. Another part of the world, the sun-drenched land of Greece, was the home of other legends about great heroes and fantastic voyages. From Greece came the *Iliad* and the *Odyssey*, stories of the Trojan War and the adventures of the hero Odysseus, who was also called Ulysses. These stories were written by the Greek poet, Homer. During the Middle Ages in Europe, "legend" often meant a collection of stories about holy persons called saints. A famous book of these tales, written in the 1200's, was the *Legenda Aurea*, "The Golden Legend," by Jacobus de Voragine. These stories about the saints were usually read aloud in monasteries and churches. Stories about nonreligious subjects later became more popular. The English poet Geoffrey Chaucer wrote the *Legend of Good Women*, about nine women noted for their suffering in the name of love. The tales of King Arthur are some of the greatest adventure legends ever told. Arthur may have been a real person, a chieftain in ancient Britain. Robin Hood and his Merry Men are the subjects of many stirring tales. Another European legend, about a mysterious ghost ship, the *Flying Dutchman*, has awed listeners for centuries.

Legends in the United States The European settlers who came to the Americas brought their own tales with them. But as the land was explored and the frontier moved west, new legends were created. Stories grew up around the lives of famous men and women. The first President of the United States, George Washington, is said to have cut down his father's cherry tree when he was a boy. When asked about it, he gave the legendary answer, "I cannot tell a lie. I did it with my hatchet." The legend of Johnny Appleseed is about a man whose real name was John Chapman. He is said to have planted apple trees all along the Ohio River valley, from Ohio to Illinois. President Abraham Lincoln became the subject of many legends. His backwoods upbringing and his great physical strength have been made into many romantic stories.

▲ *Among the most enjoyed legends of the Middle Ages were those telling of the exploits of King Arthur and his Knights of the Round Table. These stories are still popular today.*

▼ *William Tell is a legendary character. However, as with King Arthur, the legend may be based on a real person. It is possible that, around 1300, there was a Swiss hero who helped free his people from Austrian rule.*

▲ *Hiawatha says farewell to his people. According to legend, he founded the Iroquois Confederacy of tribes in New York State.*

One of the best-known legends is that of El Cid, who was said to be the chivalrous champion of Spain against the Moors. In fact, El Cid was a cruel soldier of fortune who fought for both Spaniards and Moors.

Many legendary stories were told about hard-riding westerners such as Jesse James and Billy the Kid. But of all the North American folk heroes about whom tales have been told, Davy Crockett stands a head above the rest. His real life was unusual enough to be a legend. He was a Tennessee backwoodsman, an Indian fighter, a famed hunter of bears, a United States Congressman, and a wildly funny storyteller. Davy claimed he had such a powerful grin that one flash of it could make a raccoon fall out of a tree. He is said one day to have spied a raccoon high up on a branch. Crockett smiled his terrible smile, again and again. Nothing happened. Finally, he went to look and found that the raccoon was only a giant knothole. But Davy had grinned the bark right off the tree.

Some of the most fantastic North American legends are about people who may have been imaginary. Paul Bunyan is the hero of the "tallest" (most exaggerated) stories ever. No one knows whether a lumberjack with amazing strength ever really lived in the great North Woods of America. Mike Fink was the legendary hero of the riverboat men, and Pecos Bill's adventures were described in tall stories told on the western range. Many writers have used legends they have heard. Washington Irving's *Legend of Sleepy Hollow* is a spooky story based on a tale from New York State.

Handed down from one generation to the next, legends have carried tradition, history, romance, adventure, and laughter along with them. Each new generation has added its own legends. Today, many of the old legends have been retold on films and television. Someday, legends will be told about our own time. Perhaps they will be told about the fantastic explorations of the astronauts, or about the good deeds of persons such as the German doctor Albert Schweitzer or the U.S. civil rights leader, Dr. Martin Luther King.

ALSO READ: APPLESEED, JOHNNY; ARTHUR, KING; BUNYAN, PAUL; CROCKETT, DAVY; FOLKLORE; LINCOLN, ABRAHAM; OUTLAW; ROBIN HOOD; WASHINGTON, GEORGE.

LEGISLATURE The branch of a government that has the power to make, change, or abolish that government's laws is called a legislature. Most modern legislatures are made up of representatives elected by the people.

In the past, legislatures were created as a result of disputes between early European kings and their subjects. The people wanted to take part in the making of laws that would affect them. If they were taxed, they wanted to be sure it was a fair and necessary tax. Since the thousands of citizens in one country could not spend all their time discussing government business, they elected people to do this for them.

Most modern governments have a *bicameral* (two-house) legislature. Congress, the national legislature of the United States, has two houses. The upper house (Senate) consists of two elected senators from each state. The lower house (House of Representatives) has one representative for about every 540,000 people.

Legislatures have various names, such as Congress (United States), Parliament (Great Britain), Bundestag (West Germany), Knesset (Israel), and Supreme Soviet (Soviet Union). The powers and duties of most legislatures are set up in the constitution and laws of the country. Congress gets its powers from the U.S. Constitution. State legislatures get their powers from state constitutions. Local legislative groups, such as city councils, receive their powers from documents known as charters, which must usually be approved by state legislatures.

Some nations and states have *unicameral* (one-house) legislatures. A few of these are New Zealand, Tanzania, Egypt, Israel, Sweden, and the state of Nebraska.

ALSO READ: CONGRESS, UNITED STATES; CONSTITUTION, UNITED STATES; LAW; PARLIAMENT.

LEMMING
The lemming is a small, plump rodent related to the mouse. It has thick, fluffy, brownish fur. A full-grown lemming is 4 to 5 inches (10–13 cm) long, including its stubby tail.

Lemmings are found in the cold, northern regions of the world, especially in the Scandinavian countries. They live together in large colonies dug into the earth. Grass, roots, and plants are their main food. Three times a year, female lemmings have three to eight babies. This high birth rate often leads to crowding.

A legend says that lemmings in Sweden and Norway march to the sea and drown themselves. It is not true. But thousands of lemmings do migrate every few years in search of food and more space. Many swim across lakes and rivers, and some enter the ocean, where they do drown. Because of the legend, the word "lemming" has come to mean someone who follows another without thinking.

ALSO READ: MIGRATION, RODENT.

Wood lemming

Norway lemming

▲ *The Norway lemming has long yellow-brown fur, with a bold pattern of black streaks. The wood lemming looks like a short-tailed vole.*

LEMUR The lemur is a *primate*, a relative of monkeys and apes. Monkeys may have descended from the lemur family millions of years ago. Lemurs look a little bit like monkeys, but they have long, bushy tails and foxlike faces. Most are about the size of a cat, but some are as small as squirrels.

Lemurs once lived all over the world. Today, they live only on the island of Madagascar off the southeast coast of Africa. Lemurs are very shy, gentle animals. They spend their lives in the forest, and almost never come down to the ground. During the day, most lemurs sleep in the hollow of a tree, in the shelter of rocks and sometimes in caves. They wake up when the sun goes down and spend the night hours looking for food with other lemurs. They eat leaves and twigs, fruit, insects, birds' eggs, and even birds.

The lemur's chief enemy is people. The people of Madagascar hunt lemurs with dogs. When the dogs trap a lemur in a tree, the hunters try to knock the lemur to the ground with stones. If the lemur falls out of the tree, it plays dead. Then, suddenly, it jumps up again and tries to escape by running up another tree.

ALSO READ: MADAGASCAR, MONKEY, PRIMATE.

▼ *A ring-tailed lemur rests on a branch in its native Madagascar forest. Some lemurs have weird, ghostly cries.*

Lenin's tomb, in Red Square, Moscow, is one of the Soviet Union's most honored monuments. His birthday, April 22, is a national holiday.

▲ *The Bolshevik leader V.I. Lenin, born Vladimir Ilich Ulyanov.*

LENIN, VLADIMIR ILICH
(1870–1924) The people of the Soviet Union honor the memory of V.I. Lenin just as the people of the United States honor the memory of George Washington. Lenin was the leader of the revolution that overthrew the Russian government in 1917.

Lenin was born in the Russian town of Simbirsk (now Ulyanovsk). His real name was Vladimir Ilich Ulyanov. When Lenin was a young student, he decided that the Russian government under the czar (king) was bad. The czar and his officials did little to improve the lives of the millions of poor people in Russia. Some groups of people were working secretly to change the government. Lenin's older brother, Aleksandr, belonged to one of these groups. Aleksandr was arrested in 1887, accused of plotting to kill the czar, and executed. Young Vladimir was deeply affected by this. He became involved in revolutionary activities and began to use the name Lenin to keep the czar's police from learning his real identity. He was arrested in 1895 and sent to prison for 14 months. After that, he was exiled to Siberia for three years.

Lenin's revolutionary ideas were greatly influenced by the writings of Karl Marx, a German Communist. Marx believed that the capitalist system, in which rich people owned the industries, was wrong. He wrote that the poor workers would revolt and take over the industries. He believed this would result in Communism, a system in which all the people would belong to the same social class. Lenin thought that Marx was right and that Russia would be better off under Communism.

Lenin returned from his exile in Siberia, but soon left the country. He spent most of the next 17 years in Germany and Switzerland. He met with other followers of Marx, wrote against the Russian government, and

▲ *Members of Lenin's Bolshevik party during the Russian Revolution.*

organized the Bolshevik party.

Russia fought against Germany in World War I. The Russians suffered many losses, and the government began to lose control over the people. A group of moderate revolutionaries overthrew the czar's government in March 1917. This group, led by Aleksandr Kerenski, wanted to keep Russia in the war against Germany. The Bolsheviks wanted to get out of the war. The Germans allowed Lenin to go back to Russia. When he arrived there, he led the Bolsheviks to power. Lenin became head of the new Communist government. He worked until his death to spread Communism to other countries.

ALSO READ: CAPITALISM; COMMUNISM; MARX, KARL; RUSSIAN HISTORY; SOVIET UNION; STALIN, JOSEPH; WORLD WAR I.

LENS As you read this page, move the book very close to your eyes. Can you see the words clearly? Now move the book slowly back until the words are sharp and clear. At this distance, your eyes have focused on the words. This has happened because in each of your eyes there is a lens—a clear, solid material with a smoothly curved surface. The light rays reflected from the page pass through the lens of each eye and are focused on the *retina* on the back of each eye. If the lenses in your eyes are not curved correctly or your eyes are the wrong shape, you must wear glasses to give you proper vision. Glasses are among the many types of lenses that have been invented to make things appear clearer or larger.

A lens is a transparent object that has one or more curved surfaces. Until recent times, all lenses were made of special kinds of glass. Now, many lenses are made of hard, clear plastic. A plastic lens will not break so easily as a glass lens, but its surface is more likely to get scratched.

Light rays travel through the air in a straight line. Something happens to them when they pass through a lens. The rays are *refracted* (bent) when they pass through a lens. They may bend so that they *converge* (come together), or *diverge* (spread out). A lens with a surface curved outward is called a *convex* lens. This type of lens is thicker in the middle than at the ends, and it makes light rays converge. A lens with a surface curved inward is called a *concave* lens. It is thinner in the middle than at the ends, and it makes light rays diverge.

A convex lens can be used as a burning glass. It focuses the light rays from the sun to a tiny spot, which becomes very hot. Grass, paper, or twigs can be set on fire in this way. The ancient Egyptians and Babylonians probably used convex lenses as burning glasses thousands of years ago.

A convex lens can also be used to form a *real image* of a distant scene. This type of image can be projected onto a screen. But the real image formed by a lens is upside down, or *inverted*. The lens of the human eye is a convex lens. It forms an inverted real image on the retina. However, the brain automatically reverses this image to look right-side up.

Concave lenses form *virtual images.*

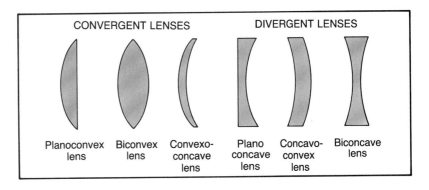

CONVERGENT LENSES | DIVERGENT LENSES

Planoconvex lens — Biconvex lens — Convexoconcave lens — Plano concave lens — Concavoconvex lens — Biconcave lens

A virtual image is right-side up, but it cannot be projected on a screen as a real image can. A concave lens cannot form a real image.

A convex lens, too, can form a virtual image. You can prove this with a magnifying glass. Look at this page through a magnifying glass. You will see an enlarged image that is right-side up. This is a virtual image. Now stand near a window and focus the lens on a sheet of white paper. The image is upside down. This is a real image.

One of the basic properties of a lens is its *focal length*. The focal length is the distance from the lens to the focal point where the light converges in a perfectly sharp focus. To measure the focal length of a magnifying glass, focus the rays from the sun onto a piece of cardboard. The distance between the lens and the cardboard is the focal length of the lens. Examine several different lenses. The more strongly curved the lens the shorter its focal length.

Some lenses are flat on one side and concave or convex on the other side. These are *plano-convex* or *plano-concave* lenses. If both sides of a lens are convex, the lens is *biconvex*; a *biconcave* lens has two concave sides. Some lenses have one side concave and the other convex. These are *concavo-convex* (meniscus) lenses. Most lenses for eyeglasses are actually concavo-convex lenses.

Very small lenses are used in microscopes. These are strongly curved and give great magnification. Telescopes use lenses, too. The largest

▼ *A magnifying glass is a lens. As light rays from an object pass through the lens, they are bent so that they come together at a point. It seems to the eye as if the light rays have come to it in a straight line, without bending. So the eye sees a much larger image of the object.*

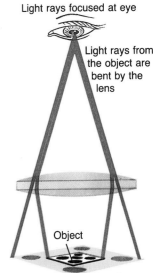

Light rays focused at eye

Light rays from the object are bent by the lens

Object

Enlarged image seen by the eye

1415

▲ *Lenses of different powers can be used in cameras. The photographs here were all taken from the same place and with the same camera, but with lenses of different power. The top picture was taken with a* wide-angle *lens to show more background. The lenses used for the bottom two were* telephoto *lenses.*

telescope lens in the world is 40 inches (101.6 cm) across. Larger lenses have not been built because it is very difficult and extremely expensive to make them.

Microscope and telescope lenses have extended our vision and shown us new worlds. Microscopes have enabled us to see bacteria. Telescopes have helped us learn about the other planets of the solar system and about the stars.

ALSO READ: EYE, GLASS, GLASSES, LIGHT, MICROSCOPE, TELESCOPE.

LEONARDO DA VINCI (1452–1519) One of the greatest artists who ever lived was also one of the world's inventive geniuses—the Italian, Leonardo da Vinci. He was born in the small village of Vinci in Tuscany during the Renaissance, a period of reawakening of interest in art, literature, and culture. Leonardo was interested in a wide range of subjects. He kept notebooks in which he asked many questions, answered those he could, and did sketches of his theories and his ideas for inventions. He even sketched his plan for an experimental airplane.

He would ask questions like "How does a heart pump blood?" or "What happens when you sneeze?" He wanted to know scientifically what lay underneath the skin he was painting. He did scientific drawings showing exposed muscles and bones.

▲ *The* Virgin and Child with St. Anne *by Leonardo da Vinci.*

Leonardo studied painting in Florence, in the studio of Andrea del Verrocchio, a leading artist of the day. At the age of 30, Leonardo went to the city of Milan, where he worked

▼ The Last Supper, *by Leonardo da Vinci.*

for some time under the sponsorship of the Duke of Milan. Leonardo was curious about the results of using different kinds of paints. Unfortunately, some of the paint experiments failed. The paint did not last, and few of Leonardo's paintings remain today. One of his best known works is his painting of *The Last Supper* (shown here). This great painting shows Christ at supper with the apostles. He has just said that one of them will betray him. Look at their reactions. Each apostle seems to be asking Christ, "Is it I, Lord?" See if you can find Judas, the one who betrayed him. This painting is famous for its use of perspective. *The Last Supper* is in poor condition today because Leonardo used his experimental paint.

Mona Lisa by Leonardo is possibly the best known and most loved painting in the world. The painting seems to glow with a mysterious light from within. Leonardo was able to get this effect by building up many layers of very thin glazes on the painting. The painting is not very large—only 30 by 21 inches (76 × 53 cm). It commands great attention at the Louvre in Paris, where it is usually exhibited. In 1962, the French loaned the painting to the United States. It was exhibited in Washington, D.C. and in New York City. At museums in both cities, thousands of people stood in line to be able to glimpse the mysterious lady.

Only one of Leonardo's paintings is not in a museum or collection in Europe. His portrait of Ginevra de Benci, an attractive young woman, hangs in the National Gallery in Washington.

Leonardo da Vinci was the most versatile (many-talented) genius of the Renaissance period. He left more than 7,000 pages of notebooks with scientific ideas and theories and sketches to go with them. The great value of his work was not really understood until the 20th century. A creator in art, a discoverer in many

▲ *Self-portrait by Leonardo da Vinci.*

branches of science, and an inventor in technology—Leonardo da Vinci could be called a "universal man."

ALSO READ: ART HISTORY, RENAISSANCE.

LESOTHO The Kingdom of Lesotho, formerly a British dependency known as Basutoland, is completely surrounded by the Republic of South Africa. (See the map with the article on AFRICA.) Unlike some African countries, Lesotho has no white landowners. The small numbers of white people who live in Lesotho are mainly European traders, missionaries, and foreign diplomats.

The climate is generally dry. Temperatures in the western lowlands range from 90° F (32° C) in the summer to 20° F (−7° C) in the winter. Lesotho has many mountains and plateaus. The snowcapped Drakensberg Mountains rise to more than 11,000 feet (3,350 m) above sealevel in the east.

In 1986, artist Lillian Schwartz used a new computer-model program to juxtapose (place side by side) the *Mona Lisa* with Leonardo's self portrait. The location of the facial features matched precisely. This suggests that the model for the *Mona Lisa* was Leonardo himself.

Leonardo Da Vinci designed an aircraft in 1483. He believed that a spiral wing, which he suggested be made of starched linen, could lift the aircraft in the same way as a spinning rotor lifts a helicopter. His machine never flew, for there was no engine to power it and, had there been, the aircraft would have spun wildly out of control because the body would have rotated in the opposite direction to the spiral wing. Modern helicopters have two rotors to prevent this happening.

LESOTHO

Capital City: Maseru (80,000 people).
Area: 11,720 square miles (30,355 sq. km).
Population: 1,700,000.
Government: Monarchy.
Natural Resources: Water and hydroelectricity, some diamonds.
Export Products: Wool, mohair, wheat, cattle, diamonds.
Unit of Money: Loti.
Official Languages: English, Sesotho.

The people of Lesotho are called *Basotho* or *Basuto*. They are descendants of Bantu-speaking peoples who came to southern Africa during the early 1600's. Most Basotho make a living by farming corn, wheat, and sorghum, or by raising sheep, goats, and cattle. Nearly half of the adults work in South Africa, in mines, industries, and farms. The country's exports are wool, mohair, livestock, and diamonds. Lesotho depends heavily on trade with South Africa. Transportation is underdeveloped. There is only one railroad: it connects the capital (Maseru) with South Africa. The country has few paved roads. But Lesotho has a good educational system, and three-fifths of the people read and write.

Lesotho came under British rule in 1868. Moshesh I, the king of the country, asked the British to protect his people from the Boers (white South Africans of Dutch descent) who wanted to settle on his land. Lesotho became independent on October 4, 1966. The government was seized in 1970 by the prime minister, Chief Leabua Jonathan. He jailed 45 political opponents, suspended the constitution, and exiled the king, Moshoeshoe II. In 1973, he allowed the king to return. In 1986, army leaders overthrew Chief Jonathan and set up a new government.

ALSO READ: AFRICA, SOUTH AFRICA.

▲ *A citizen of Lesotho in bright traditional costume.*

LETTER WRITING A letter can "speak" for you when you are miles away from someone. A letter is a message between people. Because the person who writes the letter will not be present to explain it, a letter must be written so that it can be easily understood.

When writing to friends, use the same words you would use if you were talking with them. Unless they know your address very well, you should write it at the top of your letter on the right-hand side. The date of your letter should be written below the address.

Here is a sample of a personal letter:

> 9910 Holmhurst Road
> Bethesda, Maryland 20034
> January 9, 1988
>
> Dear Greg,
>
> I looked for the belt that you thought you left at our house, but I couldn't find it. Maybe the dog buried it in the back yard!
>
> If it turns up, I will bring it with me when I visit you next weekend. Dad will drive me down on Saturday.
>
> Yours truly,
> Jeff

There are several rules to follow when writing a business letter. When addressing the envelope, the name of the person comes first if you are writing to someone in particular, and then his title, if he or she has one, such as

Mr. Thomas Wilson
Assistant Principal

On the line after this, you write the name of the company or the building, if there is a name, such as "Sandhurst Elementary School." The street number follows on the next line. Below that go the city, state, and ZIP code.

The address that is on the envelope goes on the letter, too. Here is a sample of a business letter. This one begins "Dear Sir or Madam" because no particular name is known.

9910 Holmhurst Road
Bethesda, Maryland 20034
April 17, 1988

National Wildlife Federation
1412 16th Street N.W.
Washington, D.C. 20036

Dear Sir or Madam:
I am writing a school paper on animals and birds that are becoming extinct. If you could send me a colored picture of the North American Bald Eagle, I would appreciate it very much.

Sincerely yours,
Jeffrey Naylor

A letter is a poor messenger if the writing is so messy that it is hard to read, if the words are misspelled, or if the meaning is not clear. So take care with your handwriting and grammar.

■ LEARN BY DOING

If there is something about which you feel strongly, you could write a letter to a newspaper. First you must look at the newspaper carefully to find out its address. Then send your letter to the Editor (begin the letter "Dear Editor"). If what you have to say is interesting enough, your letter may appear in the newspaper. ■

ALSO READ: COMMUNICATION, LANGUAGE ARTS.

LEWIS, JOHN L. (1880–1969)

John Llewellyn Lewis was a coal miner who became one of the best known labor leaders in the United States. He was born in Lucas, Iowa. His father was a Welsh coal miner who had settled in this country, and Lewis went to work in the Iowa mines as a young boy. His career as a labor leader began in 1906 with his first job for the United Mine Workers of America (UMW). In 1920, he became president of that union. The UMW was at that time a member of the American Federation of Labor (AFL), a large organization made up of many labor unions. Lewis thought the AFL did not fully represent the interests of industrial workers. He broke with the AFL in 1935 and persuaded several other labor-union leaders to join him in forming the Committee for Industrial Organization, later called the Congress of Industrial Organizations (CIO). He took his mine workers out of the CIO in 1942 because of disagreements with the organization's policies. The UMW rejoined the AFL for a short time, but then left to become an independent union.

Lewis was a stormy and dramatic man, with shaggy eyebrows and a fierce appearance. His efforts on behalf of the coal miners brought them much improved working conditions, increased wages, and a better way of life. Lewis was often criticized because of his demands for the coal miners. He had many battles with other union organizations and with the government. But in 1964, he was given the honored Presidential Medal of Freedom for his contributions to the welfare of mine workers.

ALSO READ: LABOR UNION.

▲ John L. Lewis, U.S. labor leader and president of the United Mine Workers of America from 1920 to 1960.

The Romans were the first great letter writers. Their able men spent years governing the distant provinces of the Empire. The only way they could learn about what was happening at home in Rome was from letters sent by friends.

▲ *Sinclair Lewis, U.S. author, with his wife, Dorothy Thompson.*

LEWIS, SINCLAIR (1885–1951)

In 1930 Harry Sinclair Lewis became the first U.S. citizen to be awarded the Nobel Prize for literature. Lewis was born in Sauk Centre, Minnesota, and was educated at Yale University. He first worked in newspapers, contributed stories to magazines, and wrote five novels, which were not widely popular. He achieved his first great success in 1920, with the publication of his sixth novel, *Main Street*.

Main Street describes the kind of middle-class life Lewis considered typical of the small American towns of the 1920's—where many people were dull, ignorant, and narrow-minded, but others were anxious to improve the quality of local life. In *Babbitt* (1922), Lewis satirizes (points out the foolishness of something by making fun of it) the life of a middle-class U.S. businessman who values only money and possessions. Lewis also wrote *Arrowsmith* (1925), about a doctor who wants to help mankind, and struggles to keep his ideals in a profession in which many others are interested only in making money.

Lewis was one of a group of writers in the early part of this century who tried to write realistically, rather than romantically, about life.

ALSO READ: LITERATURE.

LEWIS AND CLARK EXPEDITION

In 1803, the United States bought 885,000 square miles (2,292, 140 sq. km) of land from France. The total cost of the land was 15 million dollars, only about four cents an acre (10 cents a hectare)! This territory, the Louisiana Purchase, was so large that it included seven entire states and parts of six others. But very little was known about this territory. President Thomas Jefferson organized an expedition to explore the land.

He appointed two young army officers, Meriwether Lewis (1774–1809) and William Clark (1770–1838), to command the expedition. The President instructed them to find a good route to the Pacific Ocean for future settlers to travel. Lewis and Clark hired a group of 39 soldiers, three interpreters (to speak with the Indians), and a black slave. The slave, whose name was York, was really more of a valet (person's servant) for Captain Clark. Three large boats were built to carry them and their supplies up the Missouri River. After more than a year of preparation, the expedition officially started from St. Louis, Missouri, on May 14, 1804.

The explorers covered about ten miles (16 km) a day. They had several unfriendly meetings with Indians, but attacks by grizzly bears were actually more of a danger. Through the aid of the expedition's interpreters, most of the Indians they met were not only friendly, but also helpful.

In October 1804, the expedition arrived at a Mandan Indian village, in what is now North Dakota. They built Fort Mandan and stayed there for the winter. During the winter, Lewis hired a French-Canadian fur-trapper, Toussaint Charbonneau, and his wife, an Indian woman named Sacagawea, also called "Bird Woman," to act as guides and interpreters. The couple brought along their baby son on the journey.

The expedition started out again in

▼ *Lewis and Clark and their fellow adventurers on the Columbia River at the end of their long westward journey of exploration.*

April 1805. The group continued up the Missouri River into what is now Montana. There the big river divided into three branches. The explorers went up one branch in canoes as far as they could go. Then they left the river and bought horses from Sacagawea's tribe, the Shoshone Indians. The expedition continued overland across the Rocky Mountains to the Clearwater River in Idaho. They then paddled down the Clearwater to the Columbia River. They followed the Columbia to its mouth, and on November 15, 1805, they reached the Pacific Ocean. No other expedition had ever before crossed the continent north of Mexico.

The expedition spent a hard winter on the Pacific Coast, in a camp fortified against possible Indian attack. On March 23, 1806, they began their long journey home. Along the way, they split into two groups on the upper Missouri River, exploring new areas before joining again. The explorers returned to St. Louis on September 23, 1806—nearly 2½ years after they had left. Cheering crowds stood along the river to greet them. The government rewarded the members of the expedition with grants of land.

The Lewis and Clark Expedition is regarded as one of the great feats of exploration. Both Lewis and Clark kept journals during the trip, and they brought back valuable information about the geography, climate, wildlife, and Indians of the American West. The journey covered more than 8,500 miles (13,675 km). If you trace the expedition's route on the map with the article on EXPLORATION, you can understand better what a great adventure it must have been.

ALSO READ: AMERICAN HISTORY; EXPLORATION; INDIANS, AMERICAN; JEFFERSON, THOMAS; LOUISIANA PURCHASE; WESTWARD MOVEMENT.

LIBERIA The Republic of Liberia is one of the oldest independent African nations. It has never been controlled by a European country. Liberia was founded as a home for freed black slaves from the United States.

Liberia lies on the southwest tip of the bulge of West Africa. Its neighbors are the Ivory Coast to the east, Guinea to the north, and Sierra Leone to the northwest. It has a 350-mile (563 km) coastline on the Atlantic Ocean. Liberia is slightly larger than the state of Kansas. (See the map with the article on AFRICA.) Tropical rain forests cover much of the land. The rainy season lasts for eight months, when an inch (2.5 cm) or more of rain falls almost every day. Liberia has no natural harbors. However, it has a man-made harbor, a free port near Monrovia, the largest city. This port was built between 1945 and 1948 using U.S. funds. The port was turned over to the Liberian government in 1964. Ships are easy to register in

The first president of Liberia was Joseph Jenkins Roberts. He was born free in Petersburg, Virginia, and went to Liberia with his family in 1822.

LIBERIA

Capital City: Monrovia (400,000 people).
Area: 43,000 square miles (111,369 sq. km).
Population: 2,500,000.
Government: Republic.
Natural Resources: Iron ore, diamonds, gold.
Export Products: Iron ore, rubber, diamonds, lumber, coffee, cocoa.
Unit of Money: Liberian dollar.
Official Language: English.

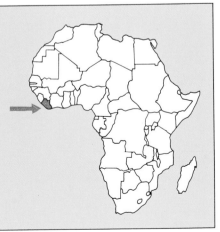

Liberia has a huge merchant marine that consists almost entirely of ships registered under a "flag of convenience." This means that almost all ships flying the Liberian flag are owned by foreign companies. These companies register their ships in Liberia because it has lower taxes and allows ship owners to pay lower wages than other countries do.

Liberia and it has the largest merchant fleet in the world.

Liberia has rich deposits of iron ore, the country's chief export. Gold and diamonds are also mined. The growing of rubber on plantations is a major business and important export. Valuable timber (mahogany and other trees) comes from Liberia's forests. Palm kernels, coffee, bananas, rice, and citrus fruits are grown.

About 90 percent of the people are descendants of black Africans who came to the area in the 1400's. They belong to about 20 tribes, follow tribal religions, and speak tribal languages. The main tribes are the Kpelle, Bassa and Kru. They mostly live and work inland. Liberians who are descendants of blacks from the United States, known as *Americo-Liberians*, speak English and live usually near the coast. Many of them work for the government. Liberia also has small groups of foreigners, such as Swiss and Lebanese.

Monrovia, the nation's capital, was the first settlement in Liberia. Freed North American blacks settled there in 1822. Monrovia was named after the United States President, James Monroe. The country became a republic on July 26, 1847, with a constitution modeled on the U.S. Constitution. In 1980, Liberia's president, William R. Tolbert, Jr., was killed during a coup d'état. A military-civilian council took control. In 1985 elections took place, but in 1990 the country was torn by civil war as two groups of rebels fought for control. The president, Samuel Doe, was killed.

ALSO READ: AFRICA.

LIBERTY BELL A huge bell, located near Independence Hall in Philadelphia, Pennsylvania, displays these words: "Proclaim Liberty throughout all the land unto all the inhabitants thereof..." Visitors touring Independence Hall can see the

▲ *The famous Liberty Bell, once housed in Independence Hall, Philadelphia.*

Liberty Bell in Liberty Bell Pavilion nearby. This bell rang out the news when the Declaration of Independence was proclaimed on July 8, 1776. The bell later became a symbol of U.S. independence from Great Britain.

The Liberty Bell weighs over 2,000 pounds (907 kg) and measures 12 feet (3.7 m) around at the rim. The original bell was brought from England in 1752. When it arrived, the bell was tested, and it cracked. Workers melted it down, and a new bell was made in 1753. Like the first bell, this one was defective. A third bell, made later that year, worked. It was hung in the wooden tower of the building now called Independence Hall. It was rung in July 1776 to celebrate the signing of the Declaration of Independence.

During the Revolution, the bell was taken down and hidden in Allentown, Pennsylvania, from 1777 to 1778. After the Revolution, the bell was returned to Independence Hall. It was rung to celebrate special occasions until 1835. In that year, it was damaged while tolling for the funeral of John Marshall, Chief Justice of the Supreme Court. Workers tried to fix the bell, but it cracked again when it was rung on George Washington's birthday in 1846.

ALSO READ: INDEPENDENCE HALL.

When bells are made, a little tin is added to molten copper. This gives the bell its mellow tone. But if too much tin is added, the bronze becomes brittle and the metal can crack. This is what happened to the Liberty Bell.

LIBRARY Books, magazines, newspapers, and other materials are collected and arranged in a library for reading and reference. By reading books in a library, it is possible to gain in knowledge and imagination and to enjoy all the cultures of the world.

Touring the Library The hours that a public library is open are often posted near the front door. Notices of story hours, movies, and exhibits shown in the library may be listed also.

The main library desk is usually near the front of the library. The reader can apply for a library card there. He or she can ask for the rules about checking out books and other materials. If the library is very large, a floor plan will probably be displayed to show where the various rooms are located.

The main room of the library also contains the card catalog, or *microfiche catalog*. The catalog is a key to the books on the shelves. It saves readers many minutes in their search for books. The microfiche viewer looks rather like a TV set. It is easy to use, once you know how. Ask a librarian to show you. There may also be file cabinets containing pamphlets, pictures, and other materials.

The largest part of the library is taken up by the shelves containing books. The juvenile, or young people's, books are usually in a separate room or rooms of the library. The tables and chairs there fit the readers who use that part of the library. The adult and the young people's books are divided into several sections. One section, often a separate room, contains the reference books. The other books are divided into two categories—storybooks, also called *fiction*, and factual books, or *nonfiction*. These books can be taken out by anyone with a library card.

Large libraries sometimes have other specialized rooms. Some have

rooms with magazines and comfortable chairs. A room may have a collection of books on a special subject, such as the history of the state. Some libraries have rooms where clubs meet and movies are shown. The library staff has rooms for offices and for preparing the books before they are put on the shelves. But these rooms are not available for readers.

Library Skills After touring the library to find where everything is located, it is a good idea to return to the catalog and learn how to use it. Every book in the library is listed in the catalog—sometimes books in neighboring libraries are listed, too. Beside the name of each book there is a number. These numbers are probably arranged by the Dewey Decimal System. This number is also on the *spine* of the book; the books are on the shelves in numerical order.

The *Dewey Decimal System* was invented by a U.S. citizen, Melvil Dewey, in 1876. It is used in libraries all over the world because it is based on numbers rather than letters or words. Numbers are the same in all countries and can be used with any language.

Dewey divided all knowledge into ten groups, called "classes." The ten classes are numbered from 000 to 900 this way:

000 General knowledge
100 Philosophy
200 Religion

▲ *A school library provides books and other printed material for both students and teachers to read. Such a room is ideal for classroom study as well as for leisure reading. Most elementary schools and high schools have a centralized library similar to this one.*

▲ *By using the index cards that catalog books by subject and by author, it is easy to find the library book you are looking for.*

The New York Public Library, which was founded in 1895, has 88 miles (142 km) of shelves. It has over 80 branches.

300 Social sciences
400 Language
500 Pure science
600 Technology
700 Arts and recreation
800 Literature
900 History

Each of the ten classes is divided into ten separate sections. This is how the class 000 is divided.

000 General works
010 Bibliography
020 Library science
030 General encyclopedias
040 General collections and essays
050 General periodicals
060 General organizations
070 Newspapers, journalism
080 Collected works
090 Manuscripts and rare books

Each of these sections is again divided into ten other sections. The number 030 is the Dewey Decimal number for encyclopedias. Using 030 as a sample, encyclopedias are divided in this way:

031 U.S. encyclopedias
032 British encyclopedias
033 German encyclopedias
034 French encyclopedias
035 Italian encyclopedias
036 Spanish encyclopedias
037 Slavic encyclopedias
038 Scandinavian encyclopedias
039 Other encyclopedias

A decimal point and other numbers often follow the first three numbers. For example, the number for Portuguese encyclopedias is 036.9. You can see from the list above that 036 is the number for Spanish encyclopedias. The number .9 was added to show that Portuguese and Spanish encyclopedias are different, although the languages are similar.

The Dewey Decimal System is constantly being changed, or added to, with the discovery of new information or inventions. For example, a new number, 629.43546, was added for books about unmanned flights to Saturn.

Both reference and circulating books are put on the shelves according to the numbers in the Dewey Decimal System. The library has signs, often clipped to the library shelves, telling where the numbers begin. In very large libraries, one of the classes may have a room to itself. For instance, a whole room may be full of history books (900). Even in smaller libraries, the books on art are sometimes separated from the others, because many art books are often oversized and need special shelves.

Reference and Specialized Material

The books in the reference section are always in the library, since they cannot be taken out by readers. Many specialized books, such as atlases and almanacs, are found in the reference section. Encyclopedias and dictionaries are an important part of the reference section, as are large volumes of technical data.

The library tries to provide as much up-to-date information as it can. Some of this is in the pamphlet file. It contains pamphlets, maps, and newspaper clippings that give more recent information than is contained in the reference books. Pamphlets, clippings, and maps, which can usually be taken out, are used often for schoolwork. Some libraries have files

▼ *The library of the German Society in Philadelphia.*

of colored pictures that may not be found in books.

Libraries may have music sections containing records or cassettes that may be taken out. Some libraries have small booths where people can listen to records or tapes they might wish to borrow. Large libraries have music scores, or sheet music, which can be used by music lovers in playing instruments or for following music while listening to records.

Many libraries have information stored on *microfilm* (tiny tapes) and *microfiche* (sheets of film with rows of images). This saves much storage space for these libraries, which have rooms in which readers can view material—newspapers, magazines, and books—on microreproductions. Ask a librarian if you wish to use one of these machines. Some libraries have information stored on computer disks or tapes—again, ask a librarian about this.

Bookmobiles The *bookmobile* is a large bus or truck full of books. It is arranged just like a normal library, with shelves of books and a check-out desk. A bookmobile goes to certain places on a regular schedule, and a librarian checks out books and receives books returned by the readers in that area.

The bookmobile began as a way to take the library into farming and mountain areas, where people lived far away from a library. However, cities have become so large that bookmobiles are now part of city library systems. They are sent to parts of the city where there are no library branches.

Librarians Today's libraries could not function without highly trained and skilled librarians. They are the people who order all the material found in the library. They have to know the community so they can buy what people want to read. They also have to find out what books are

```
J
329          Markun, Patricia Maloney
                Politics.  Illus.  by Ted Schroeder.
             F. Watts, °1970
                62p.  illus.  (A first book)




                1. Politics, Practical  2. Elections
             I. Title
```

▲ *An author card from a card catalog. The letter and numbers on the left-hand side show where you can find the book on the library shelves.*

needed to help readers in their school work, their hobbies, and their jobs. Librarians have usually taken special courses (called *library science*) in college to learn their jobs.

The work needed to keep a library useful requires librarians with specialized jobs. The first librarian a visitor sees is in the circulation department. This librarian issues the library cards and checks the books in and out. If a reader needs help in finding information about a certain subject, he or she is referred to the reference librarian. Other librarians prepare all the books for the shelves and all the pamphlets and pictures for the files. They keep the books in order, so the reader can find the ones he or she wants. Librarians also prepare the cards for the catalog and keep the catalog up to date. If you like books and enjoy meeting and helping people, you might study to become a librarian.

Early Libraries The earliest known libraries were collections of books written on clay tablets, or blocks, and on papyrus (a paperlike material), in ancient Babylonia and Egypt. The Greeks started a public library in Athens in about 540 B.C. Several public libraries were also established in Rome. One of the greatest libraries in the ancient world was in Alexandria, Egypt.

When barbarians conquered large parts of Europe, monks kept many

In its heyday ancient Rome had 28 public libraries, most of them attached to temples. They often had separate sections for Greek and Latin scrolls.

▲ *The reading room of the British Library, housed in the British Museum in London. The British Library contains more than 8½ million books. A copy of every book published in the United Kingdom is sent to it.*

The Library of Congress has 65 acres (26 hectares) of floor space and 532 miles (856 kilometres) of shelves.

are supported by private donations and by federal and state taxes.

For further information on:
History of Books and Printing, *see* EGYPT, ANCIENT; FRANKLIN, BENJAMIN; GUTENBERG, JOHANNES; JOHNSON, SAMUEL; MIDDLE AGES; MONASTERY; WEBSTER, NOAH.
Printed Matter, *see* BOOK, MAGAZINE, NEWSPAPER, PRINTING, PUBLISHING, TYPESETTING.
Reference Tools, *see* ALMANAC, ATLAS, BIBLIOGRAPHY, CARD CATALOG, DICTIONARY, ENCYCLOPEDIA, GAZETTEER, INDEX, LIBRARY OF CONGRESS, MAP, MICROFILM, RECORDING, REFERENCE BOOK.

libraries safe by storing their contents in monasteries. As Christianity spread, more books were made, since Christians wanted to be able to read the Bible themselves. The development of the printing press in the 1400's also increased the number of books available for collection in libraries. Several great university libraries were established in Europe during the 1600's and 1700's. The world-famous British Library was started in 1753. Harvard University Library, the oldest library in the United States, was founded in 1638.

The Library of Congress, the national library of the United States, was established in 1800. The Library of Congress uses a system that resembles the Dewey Decimal System, except that each major class, or group, of books is marked by a letter of the alphabet. Subdivisions are shown by an additional letter with numerals. Many special scholarly, college, and large libraries use the Library of Congress system.

Tax-supported public libraries were first established in New York in the 1800's. Free public libraries today

LIBRARY OF CONGRESS One of the largest libraries in the world started with 11 trunks of books and a case of maps. This was the beginning of the Library of Congress, in Washington, D.C. In 1800, Congress had set aside 5,000 dollars for a library of books to be placed in the new Capitol building. To begin with, 740 volumes arrived from Britain in trunks. These first books were about law and government and were for the use of the President and members of Congress.

Many people began giving books to the new library. By 1814, the library had 3,000 books. During the War of 1812, the British army invaded Washington and burned the Capitol, destroying all the library's books. After the war, Congress bought Thomas Jefferson's collection of 6,000 books to get the library started again. The number of books in the library increased greatly over the years. In 1897, the library was moved to a beautiful new building near the Capitol.

Today, the Library of Congress has about 20 million books. Some are very old and very valuable. It even has some ancient books written on stone tablets. The library has a collection of musical instruments that includes four Stradivarius violins. Early photographs, photographic equipment, and moving picture cameras are also part of the library's collection. People from all over the United States use the library for research work, but it is still primarily for the use of the members of Congress.

One of the departments of the Library of Congress is the Copyright Office. Copyrights protect authors, composers, and artists from having their creations copied. The library receives two free copies of every book copyrighted in the United States. It also prints library catalog cards for all copyrighted books printed in the United States.

ALSO READ: LIBRARY, PATENTS AND COPYRIGHTS.

LIBYA Libya is a socialist country on the northern coast of Africa. It lies between Algeria on the west and Egypt on the east. Chad and the Republic of Niger lie to the south. Libya is more than four times the size of the state of California. Tripoli is the country's capital and largest city. (See the map with the article on AFRICA.)

Most of the country lies in the hot and dry Sahara Desert. Summer temperatures inland are over 100° F (38° C). The climate along the Mediterranean coast is much cooler. The narrow coastal lands also receive as much as 20 inches (50 cm) of rain a year.

Libyans are mainly Arabs and Berbers, who follow the religion of Islam. Most are farmers who live along the Mediterranean coast. They raise dates, citrus fruits, olives, and almonds. However, the farmers depend mainly on livestock—cattle, sheep, and goats—for their income. Some Libyans fish for a living, but today about 63 out of every 100 Libyans live in cities.

Libya was for many years one of the poorest countries in Africa, mainly because of its lack of good farmland and natural resources. After World War II, a U.S. company, drilling for oil in the desert, struck water instead. They found a huge underground lake. The water has been used

▲ *The Library of Congress was founded in 1800 and housed in the Capitol. It was moved to its present site in 1897. It is the largest library in the world, containing about 20 million books (including pamphlets) and nearly 60 million other items.*

LIBYA

Capital City: Tripoli (820,000 people).
Area: 679,362 square miles (1,759,540 sq. km).
Population: 4,300,000.
Government: Jamahiriyah (a type of republic).
Natural Resources: Oil and natural gas, gypsum.
Export Products: Oil.
Unit of Money: Dinar.
Official Language: Arabic.

▲ *A productive desert oil well in the Libyan desert.*

▼ *Lichens take many shapes and forms. In fact, a lichen is not a single plant but "two in one." It consists of a fungus and an alga tightly bound together.*

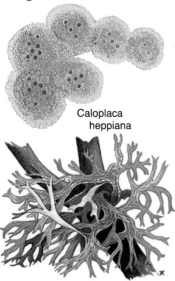

Caloplaca heppiana

Evernia prunastri

to irrigate a large part of the desert, which is now farmland. Oil was discovered in the country in 1959, and Libya is now one of the world's leading exporters of oil. Natural gas has also been found near Libya's western border. The money from oil and gas has enabled the government to build more schools, provide free health care, and improve the lives of the people.

Phoenician traders settled the northern coast of the Libyan region about 700 B.C. Rome later ruled the region for several centuries. Arabs ruled it from the 600's to the 1500's, when Libya became part of the Turkish Ottoman Empire. Libya was a colony of Italy between 1912 and the end of World War II. The United Kingdom of Libya was proclaimed in 1952. Young Libyan army officers forced out King Idris in 1969, and Colonel Muammar Qadhafi became head of the government. Libya has since aided revolutionaries and terrorists in other countries. Qadhafi has reportedly given money to terrorists in Northern Ireland, Italy, the Middle East, and Africa. One of Qadhafi's stated goals is to unite all Arabs in a single empire. In Spring 1986, the United States bombed Tripoli as a reprisal against Libya's active support of terrorism.

ALSO READ: BARBARY COAST, ISLAM.

LICE see LOUSE.

LICHEN A lichen is a plant that is made up of two kinds of other plants—an alga and a fungus—living together in a partnership. The alga makes food, some of which the fungus uses. The fungus absorbs moisture from the air, providing water the alga needs for making food.

Lichens can be found all over the world, growing on bare rocks, tree trunks, and fence posts. Lichens may be gray, blue, green, orange, yellow, or brown. There are at least 15,000 kinds of lichens. They are among the oldest plants, having first lived at least 550 million years ago.

Lichens have no roots, stems, leaves, or flowers. They consist of stalklike parts called *thalli*. These may be shaped like leaves, shells, cups, sponges, and so on. Lichens in general multiply by means of *fragments* that break off the plant and are carried away by wind or flowing water. When a fragment comes to rest, it may grow into a new lichen plant.

Some lichens are useful to people. The reindeer's food is *reindeer moss*, a kind of lichen. Eskimos and other people of the far North depend on reindeer for food and clothing. People make bread out of ground *Iceland moss*, another kind of lichen. The dye *litmus* comes from a lichen plant.

ALSO READ: ESKIMO, LAPLAND, PLANT, PLANT KINGDOM.

LIECHTENSTEIN Liechtenstein is one of the smallest countries in the world. Like a land in a fairy tale, it is ruled by a prince who lives in a beautiful old castle. The castle overlooks the small capital city of Vaduz. The Rhine River forms the country's western border with Switzerland. Austria lies to the east. The snow-capped peaks of the Alps rise in the east and south. (See the map with the article on EUROPE.)

The people of Liechtenstein are of Germanic origin. Some of them are farmers, but most now work in factories. Farmers grow grapes, corn, wheat, and potatoes. Many also raise dairy cattle. Factory workers produce textiles, ceramics, drugs, canned food, precision instruments, and optical lenses.

Liechtenstein is a prosperous country. Many international companies make their headquarters there because the taxes are low. An important source of income for Liechtenstein is the sale of its postage stamps to stamp collectors. Tourism also brings money to Liechtenstein. Visitors love the beautiful scenery. The tiny country does not have an army. During the two world wars, while armies fought in the rest of Europe, Liechtenstein and Switzerland were at peace. The two countries are good friends. Switzerland runs the postal, telegraph, and telephone systems for Liechtenstein. Swiss diplomats also represent Liechtenstein in foreign countries. The two countries use the same money, the Swiss franc.

Liechtenstein became a principality (a territory ruled by a prince) in 1719. Prince Franz Josef II has been the ruler since 1938. The prince appoints a prime minister and approves the laws made by the *Landtag* (parliament). Members of the Landtag were elected by men only until 1984, when women were given the vote.

ALSO READ: ALPS MOUNTAINS, RHINE RIVER, SWITZERLAND.

LIFE It is not easy to explain exactly what life is. It seems easy to tell whether something is alive or not. A dog and a tree are alive, and a rock is not. But we must know what else, besides appearance, sets apart the living dog from the nonliving rock.

All living things are made up of matter called *protoplasm*. Protoplasm can take in food materials and change them into more protoplasm. Protoplasm can move, grow, and rid itself of waste materials. It responds—by moving or acting in some way—to light, heat, touch, electricity, and other influences. Protoplasm can reproduce itself. It can form more protoplasm like itself.

In all living things, protoplasm is in the form of cells. A living thing may grow by increasing its number of cells (although some living things have only a single cell). Nonliving things are not made up of protoplasm. They can move only when some outside force moves them. A rock moves when something pushes it. Some nonliving things, such as crystals, seem to grow, but not by adding cells.

Where Did Life Come From? All religions teach that life was created by a divine being or force. The Old Testament of the Bible teaches that God created the world in six days.

A scientific theory about the begin-

▲ *Postage stamps for collectors are one of Liechtenstein's major exports.*

LIECHTENSTEIN

Capital City: Vaduz (4,900 people).
Area: 61 square miles (157 sq. km).
Population: 30,000.
Government: Principality.
Natural Resources: Hydroelectric power.
Export Products: Machinery, instruments, textiles, postage stamps.
Unit of Money: Swiss franc.
Official Language: German.

LIFESAVING

It has been estimated that the number of living things on Earth, not including human beings, is about 3,000 million million quintillion—3,000,000,000,000,000, 000,000,000,000, 000,000.

Scientists have calculated that the total number of living species that have ever existed on Earth is about 500 million. Today there are about 2 to 3 million.

ning of life on Earth says that life began when certain chemical compounds combined simply by chance. In the early ages of the Earth's existence, the atmosphere was made up of very different gases from the ones in it today. The energy supplied by lightning and sunlight caused some of these gases to form large molecules. The molecules included proteins and nucleic acids, which occur in protoplasm. After many millions of years these molecules combined and formed the protoplasm of the first living things.

ALSO READ: BIOCHEMISTRY, CELL.

LIFESAVING Lifesaving is the practice of saving or protecting lives, especially those of drowning persons. Lifesaving methods are today taught to as many people as possible. The next time you swim at a public pool, lake, or ocean beach, look around to

see who is guarding your life. A *lifeguard*, a person trained in lifesaving and water safety, should be there. Every year, about 9,000 persons drown in the United States and about 1,000 persons in Canada. Most of these drownings would not have happened if persons had followed basic water-safety rules.

Chapters of the American Red Cross sponsor lifesaving and water safety courses for thousands of people every year. You can take a Junior Lifesaving course at the age of 11 if you swim well. Senior Lifesaving courses are open to young people at age 15. Outstanding swimmers can train to become Water Safety Instructors at 18. Many lifeguards have completed this course. The Young Men's Christian Association (YMCA) and Young Women's Christian Association (YWCA) also have lifesaving courses for people at various age levels.

A few simple lifesaving rules should be known by everyone who

The diagrams below illustrate the chemical theory of the origin of life on Earth. Scientists suggest this took place 3,500 million years ago.

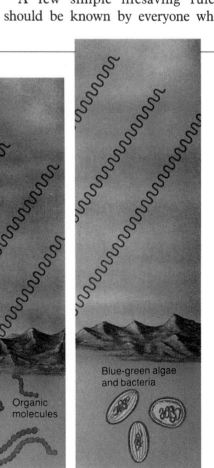

Ultraviolet radiation

Electrical storms

Organic molecules

Blue-green algae and bacteria

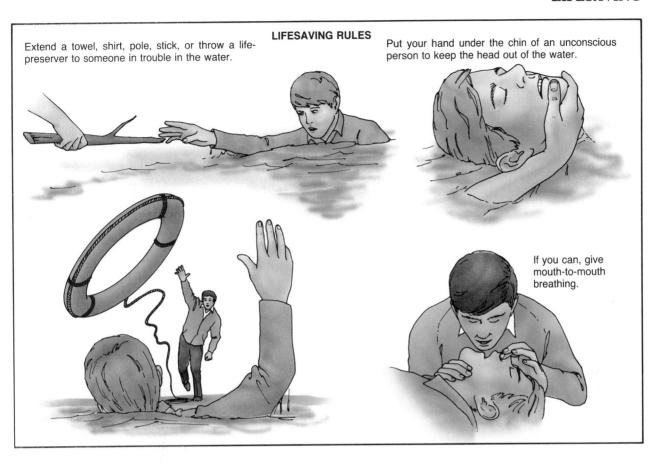

LIFESAVING RULES

Extend a towel, shirt, pole, stick, or throw a life-preserver to someone in trouble in the water.

Put your hand under the chin of an unconscious person to keep the head out of the water.

If you can, give mouth-to-mouth breathing.

goes swimming, boating, surfing, or waterskiing. If you ever see a person struggling in deep water, your first thought would be to jump in and go to him or her. That is actually the last thing to do—and then only if you are a very good swimmer. The person may panic, try to climb up on you to get above water to breathe, and pull you both under. If the person is close by, hold out your hand or extend a towel, shirt, stick, pole, oar, or similar object. Be sure to lie down so as not to be pulled into the water. If the person is farther out, throw out a life preserver, raft, board, or any other object that will float. If you have a boat, use it to rescue the person.

If you are swimming in shallow water and see someone unconscious underwater, put your hand under the person's chin and lift his or her head out of the water. Then call for help. Remember that drowning happens very quickly, so it is important to do this as fast as possible. This simple assist is taught in beginning swim-ming classes by the American Red Cross. Several children have saved the lives of fellow swimmers by knowing it.

A swimmer who becomes unconscious and stops breathing must be helped to start breathing again by *artificial respiration*. Mouth-to-mouth breathing by a trained person is often used. Most pools and supervised beaches have mechanical resuscitators.

Rules for Swimming Safety Good swimmers say, "No one swims alone." Even in a pool or at a beach with a lifeguard, it is a good idea to go swimming with a friend. You and your friend can keep a minute-to-minute check on each other at a crowded waterfront. If you do not know how to swim, stay in shallow water. If you are learning to swim it is a good idea to walk out, then swim back. By doing this you won't find yourself in deep water without knowing it.

The most powerful sources of light are lasers. They can produce a beam so intense that it will cut through steel. Astronomers have reflected a laser beam off the moon back to Earth in order to measure the moon's exact distance from Earth.

▲ *This bicyclist is using fluorescent clothing and fittings so that he will show up clearly in drivers' headlamps. Fluorescence is a type of* luminescence. *In luminescent materials, the atoms are excited when light hits them. Instead of just reflecting light, they absorb its energy temporarily. When they release the energy it is in the form of light of a different character.*

Don't float out into deep water on a rubber raft or inner tube. Sometimes the air leaks out. Don't swim in dirty water, or in any place where you don't know how deep the water is. Don't swim at night in unlighted water. If you suddenly needed help, no one could see you. Be careful when swimming in rough water. You can be knocked around in the breaking waves.

Wait a half-hour after eating before going into the water. This will help prevent muscle tightness, or *cramps.* If you get a cramp, try to stretch, or change the way you are swimming. If the cramp does not go away, float until someone can help you.

Don't swim in areas where people are surfing or riding in motorboats. If you are going out in a boat, make sure there is a life preserver for each person. If your boat turns over in deep water, or starts to fill with water, hang on to it. It will float. Last of all, learn to swim as well as you possibly can.

ALSO READ: ARTIFICIAL RESPIRATION, BOATS AND BOATING, FIRST AID, SAFETY, SWIMMING.

LIGHT You know that when the sun shines during the day, everything is visible as far as the eye can see. You also know that after the sun has set, the night is dark. This happens because the sun is the most powerful source of light for the Earth. A burning match, a bonfire, or a lighted electric bulb are other sources of light. But there would be no matches, fires, or domestic electricity if the sun were not shining on the planet Earth. The fuels used to provide light and electricity—wood, coal, and oil, for instance—come from plants and animals, which all need the sun's light to live. Without the sun, there would be no light on Earth, and therefore no life at all.

The sun is a star, about 93 million miles (150 million km) away from the

Earth. Light from the sun travels this great distance in only eight minutes. It moves at the tremendous speed of about 186,300 miles (about 300,000 km) a second. This is a huge speed: light could go around the Earth more than seven times in one second!

Movement of Light Light travels in the form of waves; these move in much the same way that waves travel in water. Light waves are a tiny fraction of an inch in length. Light usually travels through air in a straight line. You can see this by looking at the straight beam of a flashlight. But you could not see the beam if it were not for the fact that light can be *reflected*. Light rays are reflected when they "bounce off" an object. You see the beam from the flashlight because the light is reflected by particles of dust or moisture in the air. You can see sunbeams in the sky for the same reason. In fact, you see most things because of reflection of light.

When light rays hit some objects, they are not only reflected but may also pass through the objects. Anything that allows light to pass through it is *transparent.* Clear glass, water, and air are transparent. Anything that breaks up the light as it passes through is *translucent.* You cannot see clearly through a translucent object, such as a pane of frosted glass. (Your skin is translucent, too. Try some experiments with a flashlight in a darkened room.) Anything that does not allow light to pass through it is *opaque.* A stone wall is opaque.

When light passes through substances, including air, its speed is slowed down. This causes light rays to be *refracted* as they pass from one substance to another. This means the light rays are bent. You can see this by looking at a glass of water that has a straw in it. The straw seems to bend at the surface of the water, because light reflected from the straw changes direction as it passes from the water into the air. *Lenses* can control the

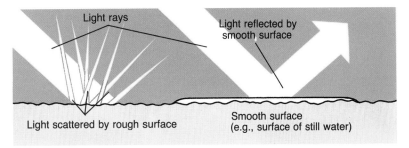

Light rays

Light reflected by smooth surface

Light scattered by rough surface

Smooth surface (e.g., surface of still water)

bending of light rays to suit different purposes. The lens of a telescope can make distant objects appear near. In astronomy, a telescope is used to make things appear brighter: all the light that reaches the big lens at the front is concentrated into the very small lens at the back. The lens on a microscope can make tiny objects, invisible to the naked eye, appear large enough to be studied. The lens on a camera is used to *focus* images (make them appear clear and sharp) on the film in the camera. If you do not see things sharply and clearly, you need glasses. The lenses that are correct for you are made to bend the light rays just enough to correct your vision.

Sunlight appears to be white, but when it is refracted through a wedge-shaped piece of glass called a *prism*, a rainbowlike band comes from the glass. This band of light is called a *spectrum*. It shows that white light is made up of different colors. Each color has a different wavelength, and bends a different amount. Violet, at one end of the spectrum, has the shortest wavelength and bends the most. Red, at the other end of the spectrum, has the longest wavelength and bends the least. Between red and violet are indigo, blue, green, yellow, and orange. A rainbow may appear in

▼ *Straight objects seem bent in water because light rays bend when they pass from water to air.*

the sky during or after a rainstorm because the tiny drops of water in the air act as prisms to bend the sunlight into the colors of the spectrum. When you direct a fine spray from a garden hose in the sunlit air, you may see a rainbow in the spray.

Sources of Light Many things can be heated to produce a source of light. The color of the light given off depends on the temperature and on what is being heated. The metal filament in an electric lamp glows white because the current heats it to a very high temperature. The flame of a candle looks yellow, because the temperature is much lower than in the electric lamp. Many of the things you see are not sources of light. They are *nonluminous*—they only reflect light. But some things that reflect light seem to be luminous. The moon is a good example of this. It seems to shine, but, in fact, it reflects light from the sun. Some road signs contain many beads that seem luminous when the headlights of an automobile shine on them. But these beaded signs only reflect the light from the headlights, which are the real source of the light. There are two units used to measure light. The intensity of a lightsource is measured in *candelas*, and the illumination of a surface is measured in *lux*. A 60-watt light bulb has an intensity of 50 candelas, and it lights up a surface 1 m (39½ in) away with an illumination of 50 lux, which is bright enough for reading. If you are reading this page near a window on a clear day, you are getting about 1,000 lux on the page. Your eyes adjust to different levels of illumina-

▲ *All the objects around you reflect light, but some do so better than others. When light hits a rough object, the rays are scattered in many directions. Wherever you stand, only a few of the reflected light rays will enter your eyes. When a beam of light hits a smooth object, such as the surface of still water, all the rays are reflected off it in the same direction. If you stand in the right place, you will see the object as shiny.*

▲ *Ordinary white light is actually a mixture of light of many different colors. To show this, paint a disk with the colors of the rainbow. Stick a pin through the center, and then spin the disk like a top. As the disk spins the colors will merge together to make white.*

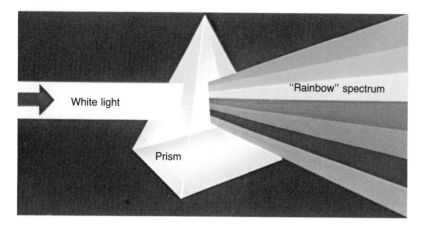

"Rainbow" spectrum

White light

Prism

▲ *White light can be split into the colors of the rainbow (the* spectrum) *by shining it through a prism. The prism bends* (refracts) *light of different colors by a different amount. In fact, the spectrum contains not just seven colors but billions of colors. The study of spectrums is called* spectroscopy.

The shortest light waves that we can see are blue and violet. The longest light waves we can see are red. But there are other waves shorter than violet and longer than red that we cannot see but some animals can. Bees and ants see colors beyond violet, but pure red is no color to a bee. It sees red objects as black.

tion. Photographers may use light-meters to measure the amount of light that is reflected from the object they want to photograph. By knowing the amount of light available, the photographer can widen or narrow the lens opening on the camera and control the amount of time the shutter should remain open to allow the right amount of light to strike the film. (Many cameras have automatic light-meters.)

■ LEARN BY DOING

A simple experiment proves that light rays can be refracted. Put a quarter in an empty, deep bowl. Put the bowl on a table in front of you. Move the bowl away from you until you can no longer see the quarter over the rim of the bowl. Now, without moving your head, slowly pour water into the bowl. Suddenly, you will be able to see the quarter again. The water in the bowl has reached a point where it bends the light rays reflected from the quarter so that they are directed to your eyes. ■

For further information on:
Characteristics of Light, *see* ATMO-SPHERE, AURORA, COLOR, DAY AND NIGHT, ECLIPSE, RAINBOW, SPEC-TRUM, WAVE.
Science and Light, *see* ASTRONOMY; EDISON, THOMAS ALVA; EINSTEIN, ALBERT; EYE; RELATIVITY; SIGHT.
Sources of Light, *see* ASTRONOMY, POWER, FIRE, LASERS AND MASERS,

STAR, SUN.
Uses of Light, *see* CAMERA, GLASSES, KALEIDOSCOPE, LENS, LIGHTHOUSE, LIGHTING, LASERS AND MASERS, MATCH, MICROFILM, MICROSCOPE, MIRROR, PHOTOELECTRICITY, PHOTO-SYNTHESIS, TELESCOPE, X RAY.

LIGHTHOUSE Before the days of radio and radar, ships sometimes were wrecked at night on rocky coasts. Sailors feared getting too close to land at night, because the persons at the helm, steering the ship, could not see dangerous rocks or sandbars. A way of warning ships was needed, so the lighthouse came into being.

The first known lighthouses were built in Egypt about 300 B.C. The great lighthouse of Pharos guided ships that were sailing near Alexandria at night. Priests kept bright fires burning at the top of the lighthouse. Sailors saw the fires and knew where the land was.

The most common lighthouse in modern times is a round building built of rock, brick, concrete, or iron. At the top of the lighthouse is a powerful lamp. Even in bad weather, the light can be seen for several miles. The light spins in a circle, slowly moving its bright beam across the sky. Most lighthouses have shields that keep the light from shining on land. But each time the light comes around to the water side, sailors can see it.

Until the middle of the 1800's, light was provided by candles or coal-oil lamps. The first lighthouse with an electric light was South Foreland Light, England, in 1858. About the same time, lighthouses began using a lens system to make the beam stronger.

Today, lighthouses still in operation are equipped with *radio beacons* that send out signals to guide ships. Many modern lighthouses operate automatically, without requiring people to look after them, and some are nuclear-powered. Old lighthouses are often preserved as historic monuments.

ALSO READ: SHIPS AND SHIPPING.

LIGHTING With only a touch of your finger on the light switch, you can have light in a dark room at night. But not many decades ago, homes did not have electric light.

Once people could work and play only in daylight, and went to bed when the sun went down. Then they learned to burn bundles of rushes to light their living places. Archeologists (scientists who study past human cultures) have found lamps from around 1000 B.C. The lamps were made with woven *wicks*, or strings, which absorbed oil, and drew it toward the lighted end of the wick. Roman lamps burned olive oil. The Dutch "Betty" lamp, made of iron, was brought to North America by the Pilgrims. It burned whale oil.

Candles, which are wicks dipped into tallow or beeswax many times, were used through the 1700's for lighting. People still use candles today for special lighting.

In 1784, a Swiss, Aimé Argand, invented a lamp with a space for oil and a circular wick that gave more light than a string wick. Later, he added a glass chimney for a brighter glow.

North Americans used gas light in the early 1800's. At first just the bluish flame provided the light. Then a mantle, a small net cup that glowed in the flame, was added to give more light. Kerosene was a popular and inexpensive fuel for lamps after 1860.

Electric Light Thomas A. Edison, a U.S. inventor, wanted to make a safe electric lamp to replace gas lamps. Other persons had operated electric lamps for short times before the materials burned up. Edison found *carbon* was the material to use in a light. It could be heated to give off light, but would not burn to an ash. Edison ran an electric lamp for 40 hours in 1879 and proved that electric lighting was possible. Edison's first bulb used a filament made of sewing thread covered with carbon. He tried to use paper, hair, wood, cardboard, and grasses in making the carbon thread. One day he tried a splinter from a bamboo fan he

▲ *Lighthouses have been in use for thousands of years.*

▼ *Different types of lighting, over the ages, from the simple Roman oil lamp to the modern fluorescent tube.*

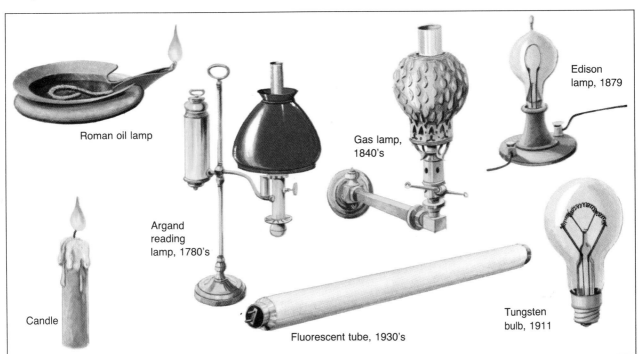

Roman oil lamp

Candle

Argand reading lamp, 1780's

Gas lamp, 1840's

Fluorescent tube, 1930's

Edison lamp, 1879

Tungsten bulb, 1911

▲ *Museums and art galleries depend on precision spot lighting to highlight individual items and enhance cabinet displays.*

When Thomas Edison's first generating plant opened in 1882 it supplied electricity to light 2,323 lamps. By 1884 it was lighting over eleven thousand lamps. By 1885 there were about a quarter of a million electric lamps in use in the United States.

became popular after 1938, in stores, offices and schools. It gives more light for less electricity and looks almost like daylight.

Sir William Ramsay discovered a new gas in 1898. He called it neon. Tubes filled with neon glow very brightly when a current of electricity goes through them. They make the brilliant red lights used in advertising signs. Other gases make the blue and green ones. Lamps filled with sodium make a bright orange light and are used on busy highways and at dangerous intersections.

Look around the room when you and your family are reading or writing. See if each person has enough light. If you are right-handed, you should have light coming over your left shoulder. If you are left-handed, you need light over your right shoulder. Be sure the bulb is strong enough to give a good light.

ALSO READ: CANDLE; EDISON, THOMAS ALVA; ELECTRIC APPLIANCE; FLUORESCENCE; INTERIOR DECORATION; KEROSENE; LIGHT; LUMINESCENCE.

was holding. The bulb burned for 400 hours.

Bulbs by themselves would have been of little use, but Edison invented electric generators to send *current* around the cities. In 1882, the generators he designed were in use in New York at the first city power station. Ten city blocks could be lighted. The public saw electric lighting at the Chicago World's Fair of 1893. By 1900, many homes had made the change from gas lighting to electricity.

Edison kept improving and changing electric lighting. Tungsten filaments replaced carbon in 1907. Then gases were sealed into the bulbs to brighten the light. In 1926, the bulbs were frosted inside to lessen the glare. Indirect lighting was introduced in 1934, and then three-strength bulbs.

Fluorescent and Neon Fluorescent lights have no filaments. The glass tubes are coated on the inside with substances called *phosphors*. Then the tube is sealed and filled with a vapor, such as mercury vapor. Electricity passes through the vapor and makes the phosphors glow with strong, steady light. This form of lighting

▼ *Lighting in the 17th century involved elaborate candle lighters and snuffers. The candles on this one chandelier in the Versailles Palace, France, must have taken some time to light—and put out.*

▲ *The vivid orange-red glow of neon tubes has been much used on shops, hotels and offices for advertising since the 1920's.*

LIGHTNING AND THUNDER

A flash of bright light spears its way across the sky. Then a crackling, rumbling sound occurs. The flash is lightning, a giant spark. The sound is thunder, caused by the lightning. The large spark of lightning is electricity moving very rapidly between a cloud and the Earth, between two clouds, or between two parts of the same cloud. Clouds in which lightning forms are called *thunderclouds*. Rapidly rising air currents containing water drops or ice particles cause positive electric charges to collect mainly at the top of the cloud and negative charges in most of the rest of the cloud. The positive charges in the cloud and the negative charges in another cloud, within the same cloud, or on Earth, attract (pull toward) each other.

When a very large number of positive charges collect at the top of the cloud, they become strong enough to force their way through the air. They jump to a negative charge, making a huge spark, called a lightning bolt.

Lightning has several forms. *Forked*, or *chain*, lightning is the crooked lightning you see zigzagging across the sky in any thunderstorm. *Sheet*, or *heat*, lightning lights up the whole sky. It has no special shape. Sheet lightning is the light from a chain lightning flash that occurs very far away. *Ball* lightning is rather different—in fact, until a few years ago scientists did not believe it existed! It takes the form of a brightly shining ball, perhaps a few inches across. It travels eerily around, hissing, until it suddenly disappears or explodes.

A flash of lightning heats the air around it. The heated air spreads out, forming an air wave (sound wave). The lightning bolt is a zigzag. Each part of the zigzag bolt causes an air wave in a slightly different direction. The air waves pass you one after another, so you hear thunder as a series of rumbles. If you are caught outdoors in a thunderstorm, stay away from high objects because they attract lightning. Do *not* use an umbrella, because its metal part also attracts lightning. Lie down on the ground if you cannot find shelter.

ALSO READ: CLOUD, ELECTRICITY, SOUND, WEATHER.

When a lightning flash happens between a cloud and the ground, several things occur. An electric current of some 10,000 amperes passes between the ground and the cloud. This enormous current travels through a band of air about an eighth of an inch (3 mm) across. The air becomes intensely hot at around 54,000°F (30,000°C) and glows with a blinding white light. It is the hot air expanding suddenly at the speed of sound that causes the thunder.

▼ *A streak of lightning flashes over a harbor at night. Bolts of lightning were once thought to be hurled by gods like Jupiter and Thor, but we now know that they are gigantic electric sparks in the atmosphere.*

LILIUOKALANI, LYDIA KAMEKEHA (1838–1917)

The song "Aloha Oe" ("Farewell to Thee") was written by Liliuokalani, the last ruler of the kingdom of Hawaii. She was born in Honolulu and attended the Royal School. Liliuokalani married a U.S. citizen, John Dominis. Her brother, King David Kalakaua, died in 1891. Liliuokalani became queen. She tried to defend her power against U.S. plantation owners in Hawaii who wanted to control the islands. But in January 1893, the leaders of this group rebelled and took over the government. U.S. Marines landed to prevent any fighting, and the rebels made Liliuokalani give up her throne. The following year, Hawaii became a republic.

Liliuokalani asked President Grover Cleveland to help her regain her throne. But the plantation owners who governed Hawaii decided that the islands should become a part of the United States. They knew this would give them a good market for their crops. The United States annexed (took control of) Hawaii in 1898.

ALSO READ: HAWAII.

▲ *Queen Liliuokalani of Hawaii.*

LIMERICK A limerick is a short poem, usually humorous. It always has five lines. The first two lines rhyme. The third and fourth lines rhyme with each other. And the fifth line rhymes with the first two. Each limerick tells a little story. Here is a limerick about a tiger:

> There was a young man from the city,
> Who met what he thought was a kitty.
> He gave it a pat,
> And said, "Nice little cat."
> They buried his clothes, out of pity.

No one knows for sure where the limerick began. Some sources say that even in ancient Greece, people made up limerick-like verses. Many people throughout the centuries have written limericks. Here is a limerick by President Wilson:

> As a beauty I'm not a great star,
> There are others more handsome by far,
> But my face, I don't mind it,
> Because I'm behind it,
> 'Tis the folks in the front that I jar.

The name "limerick" probably came from Ireland, where a county and seaport are both named Limerick. One story says that a band of soldiers, the Irish Brigade, used to sing limericks at their gatherings. Each verse would end with a chorus that went, in part, "Won't you . . . Come all the way up to Limerick?"

Edward Lear, a British poet who wrote and illustrated nonsense rhymes, made the limerick so popular that his name is almost always associated with it. Here is a limerick by Lear:

> There was a young lady of Wilts,
> Who walked up to Scotland on stilts;
> When they said it is shocking
> To show so much stocking,
> She answered, "Then what about kilts?"

Around the beginning of the 1900's, many newspapers in England ran contests for the best examples of limericks. Try making up a funny limerick yourself!

ALSO READ: LEAR, EDWARD; POETRY.

LIMPET see SNAILS AND SLUGS.

LINCOLN, ABRAHAM (1809–1865)

Few persons have had greater influence on U.S. history than Abraham Lincoln. He served as President during the Civil War, and took the firm steps necessary to prevent the North and South from becoming two separate nations. His kindness, wit, and ability to express great truths in

A "nugget" in limerick style
Is merely a matter of guile;
The rhyme to this line
Can be nine, fine, or mine,
The last one is suitably vile.

words that everyone could understand have made "Honest Abe" one of our most beloved leaders.

Early Life Lincoln was the 16th President, and the first one who did not start life in one of the 13 original states. He was born in a log cabin near what is now Hodgenville, Kentucky. He moved with his parents and an older sister, Sarah, to the backwoods of Indiana when he was seven. His mother, Nancy, died two years later. His father, Tom, was a carpenter and farmer, and was very poor. Conditions improved for the Lincoln children after Tom married his second wife, Sarah Bush Johnson, who took a special interest in young Abe. She encouraged him to educate himself, even though he had less than a year's schooling. She could neither read nor write, but she owned several books that Abe began to study. Abe helped support the family by splitting logs for fence rails and working at other odd jobs during the 14 years that the Lincolns lived in Indiana. The family left Indiana for Illinois when Abe was 21, and he helped his father set up a new farm there.

Lincoln then set out on his own. He lived for six years (1831–1837) in the village of New Salem, Illinois. He clerked in a store for a while, was appointed postmaster, served in the Black Hawk War (1832), and studied law in his spare time. An old legend, revived in books and poems, tells that Abe fell in love with a New Salem girl named Ann Rutledge during this time. They were good friends, and he was filled with sorrow when she died in 1835.

The awkward, rather homely young Lincoln, who was well over six feet (1.83 m) tall, was a skillful wrestler and liked to tell funny stories. He made friends easily, and was elected to the Illinois legislature in 1834. Three years later, he received his license to practice law, and moved to Springfield, where he became a successful lawyer and one of the town's leading citizens. He married an ambitious young woman, Mary Todd, who boasted that she intended to help

▲ *President Lincoln entering Richmond, the Confederate capital, in 1865, a few days before Lee surrendered to Grant at the end of the Civil War.*

"Honest Abe" won his nickname in New Salem. He and a man named William Berry bought a store there. When Berry died and the business failed, Lincoln worked for several years to pay back the store's debts of about $1,000.

ABRAHAM LINCOLN
SIXTEENTH PRESIDENT   MARCH 4, 1861–APRIL 15, 1865

Born: February 12, 1809, near Hodgenville, Kentucky
Parents: Thomas and Nancy Hanks Lincoln
Education: Self-educated
Religion: No special denomination. Attended Presbyterian Church during his Presidency.
Occupation: Lawyer
Political Party: Republican
State Represented: Illinois
Married: 1842 to Mary Todd (1818–1882)
Children: 4 sons (2 died in childhood, another at age 18)
Died: April 15, 1865, Washington, D.C.
Buried: Oak Ridge Cemetery, Springfield, Illinois

► *Abraham Lincoln was a deeply religious man. Here, he is reading the Bible to his son Thomas (nicknamed "Tad").*

▼ *President Lincoln meeting with General Sherman, General Grant, and Admiral Porter in March 1865, to discuss the peace terms to be offered to the South.*

her husband become President of the United States.

Political Career Lincoln was elected to Congress in 1847. His two years in Washington were a disappointment, however. Because he had spoken out against the government's policy in going to war against Mexico, he was not popular in his home district. He did not run for a second term in Congress, but returned to his law practice in Springfield. He seemed to lose interest in politics until Congress passed the Kansas-Nebraska Act in 1854.

This new law made it possible for people to own slaves in the new western territory being opened to settlers.

Slavery was then legal in the Southern states, but Lincoln felt territory that was still free must be kept that way. In 1856, he joined the new Republican Party, which had been formed to fight the spread of slavery. The Republicans in Illinois nominated him for the U.S. Senate in 1858. That summer he and Stephen A. Douglas, the nominee of the Democratic Party, held debates in seven different Illinois towns.

Douglas defended the Kansas-Nebraska Act. Lincoln opposed it. In one debate he summed up what he thought slavery meant. One race of people, he said, had no right to make slaves of another race and "live by the fruits of their labor."

Lincoln lost the election for the Senate, but his speeches during the Lincoln-Douglas debates helped make him nationally known. He was nicknamed the "Railsplitter," because of his days spent splitting logs for fence rails. The Republican Party nominated him for President in 1860, and he won the election easily. Many Southerners were afraid to live under a President who was so firmly against slavery. Several Southern states had *seceded* by the time Lincoln was inaugurated. They left the Union and formed a new nation, which they called the Confederate States of America.

Lincoln thought that no state had the legal right to break up the Union. He believed that people in a democracy must be willing to obey the laws and live under the officials that most of the voters want. His main purpose in fighting the Civil War (1861–1865) was to keep all of the states together as one country.

Lincoln issued the Emancipation Proclamation on January 1, 1863, while war was still raging. This document stated that the slaves in states or parts of states then in rebellion against the government should be "thenceforward, and forever free." He defined democracy later that year in his famous Gettysburg Address. He said it should be "government of the people, by the people, for the people." The war was being fought, he said, to test whether a nation founded on democratic principles "can long endure."

Victory was in sight by the time Lincoln began his second term as President in March 1865. In his Second Inaugural Address, he said that America's next task was "to bind up the nation's wounds . . . and to do all which may achieve and cherish a just and lasting peace. . . ." He wanted to make it easy for the states that had seceded to take their places again in the Union, but he did not live to carry out his plans. He attended a play at Ford's Theatre in Washington, D.C., on the evening of April 14, 1865. There, he was shot by John Wilkes Booth, a successful actor half crazed with disappointment because the South had lost.

Abraham Lincoln died the following morning. "Now he belongs to the ages," said Secretary of War Edwin M. Stanton. A special train took Abe Lincoln's body back to Illinois for burial. Mourners lined the tracks in the states along the way to honor the martyred President. Lincoln's memory is still revered today. Every year thousands of people climb the marble steps of the Lincoln Memorial in

▼ *Lincoln's writing desk complete with his stovepipe hat, reading spectacles, and pipe.*

Washington, D.C. They look up at the gigantic statue of the seated Lincoln and read the words inscribed on one of the marble walls:

In this temple
as in the hearts of the people
for whom he saved the Union
the memory of Abraham Lincoln
is enshrined forever.

ALSO READ: ASSASSINATION; CIVIL WAR; CONFEDERATE STATES OF AMERICA; DOUGLAS, STEPHEN A.; EMANCIPATION PROCLAMATION; GETTYSBURG ADDRESS; ILLINOIS; PRESIDENCY.

LINDBERGH, CHARLES AUGUSTUS (1902–1974)

In 1927, a small single-engine airplane named the *Spirit of St. Louis* took off from Roosevelt Field on Long Island, New York, and headed out over the Atlantic Ocean. Just 33 hours and 39 minutes later, the plane landed at LeBourget Airport near Paris, France. It had flown 3,600 miles (5,790 km). The date was May 21, 1927. The news spread rapidly around the world. Charles Lindbergh had become the first person to fly alone across the Atlantic without stopping. Fliers had crossed the Atlantic before—but never alone.

Lindbergh decided to make the flight when a wealthy New Yorker offered a $25,000 prize to the first person to make a solo, nonstop flight from New York to Paris. He flew the *Spirit of St. Louis* on a practice run from San Diego, California, to New York City on May 10, 1927. This trip took 21 hours and 45 minutes. It set a new record for flight across the continent.

Charles Lindbergh was born in Detroit, Michigan, and grew up in the small town of Little Falls, Minnesota. He liked working on engines. At the age of nine, he could take an engine apart, fix it, and put it back together. Lindbergh worked as an airplane mechanic and stunt man at air shows and

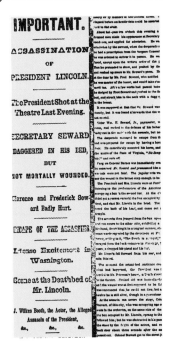

▲ *Newspapers throughout the land brought the news of the President's assassination to a shocked nation.*

Although Lindbergh was the first pilot to make a solo trans-Atlantic flight, 78 other fliers had made the crossing, but in crews.

▲ *Charles A. Lindbergh standing beside the airplane in which he made the first solo nonstop flight across the Atlantic Ocean.*

earned enough money to buy his own airplane at age 19. In school, he did especially well in mechanics. When he became an Army flying cadet, he was first in his class.

Lindbergh was only 25 years old when he made his historic nonstop flight from New York to Paris. Overnight, he became a world hero, and was awarded the Congressional Medal of Honor. The next year (1928) he flew to Central America, carrying the first airmail. He and his wife, the author Anne Morrow Lindbergh, flew to the Orient (Asia) in 1931. Their first child, a son, was kidnapped and killed the next year. In 1954, Lindbergh received the Pulitzer Prize for his book *The Spirit of St. Louis* (1953). Charles Lindbergh's airplane, *Spirit of St. Louis*, is now in the National Air Museum of the Smithsonian Institution, Washington, D.C.

ALSO READ: AIRLINE, AIRPLANE, AIRPORT, ATLANTIC OCEAN, AVIATION, WORLD WAR II.

▲ *Japan National Railway Company's model of the new high-speed monorail train that runs between Tokyo and Osaka. The train is powered by a linear motor. You can see the electromagnets just beneath the rail.*

LINEAR MOTOR Most types of electric motor give *rotary* power: they make a shaft or a wheel spin. But some types provide movement in a straight line. These are called linear motors.

A simple type was invented by the British scientist Sir Charles Wheatstone in 1845. Imagine a long row of electromagnets, and an iron object. If

you switch on one magnet the object will move toward it. If you switch that magnet off, but switch on the next one, the object will move again. If you do this along the whole row of magnets, the object will move the whole distance.

Linear motors are used in factories and in some single-rail (monorail) transportation systems. An exciting future possibility is that huge linear motors may be built on the moon. They would be able to make containers of the moon's valuable ores go very quickly—quickly enough to be launched all the way into space. There the ores could be processed easily and cheaply by people working in space factories, before being sent on to Earth.

LINNAEUS, CAROLUS (1707–1778) Karl von Linné devised the *binomial* (two-name) system of scientific names for plants and animals. In this system, every type of living thing is given a name in Latin. Each name has two parts. The first part names the *genus*, or group that an animal or plant belongs to. The second part names the exact *species*, the exact kind of plant or animal within the genus. For example, the wolf's scientific name is *Canis lupus*. *Canis* means "dog." This tells us that a wolf belongs to the dog group. *Lupus* means "wolf," and tells the species of dog.

He was born in Rashult, Sweden, and attended medical school. While a student, he ran a small botanical garden. He took careful notes describing the plants in this garden. His notes became the basis for his system of names.

In 1732, he was given some money by the Swedish Royal Society of Science. He used it to take a walking trip through Lapland, collecting plants. Afterwards he went to the Netherlands, where he finished his medical studies. When he returned to Sweden, he was made professor of botany and natural science at Uppsala University and became physician to the king. In his lifetime, he wrote 180 books. He wrote them in Latin, using the name Carolus Linnaeus—the name by which he is now best known.

ALSO READ: ANIMAL KINGDOM, BIOLOGY, BOTANY, PLANT KINGDOM.

LION The lion has long been known as the "king of the beasts" because of its dignified appearance, its strength, and its size. The lion is the largest member of the cat family, except for tigers. A full-grown male lion is about 3 feet (91 cm) high at the shoulder, about 7 feet (213 cm) long, and may weigh up to 500 pounds (227 kg). It has a long tail that is tipped with a tuft of dark hair. Many lions may reach a length of more than 10 feet (3 m) from the tip of the nose to the end of the tail. Female lions (*lionesses*) are slightly smaller than the males.

The adult male lion has a long, shaggy growth of hair, called a *mane*, around its head, neck, and shoulders. Young males, or *lionets*, begin to grow manes at about three years of age. The color of the mane usually matches the lion's coat, which is all one color, varying from silvery-gray to dark brown.

A lioness produces 2 to 6 cubs in a litter. A cub is about the size of a house cat and has similar streaks and spots. The cubs are very playful, behaving like kittens. They often wrestle with each other. The cubs stay with the lioness until they are about two years old. They are completely mature at the age of 4 or 5, and will live for 15 to 20 years. Lions live in a *pride*, or group, which may consist of a few males and many females and cubs. The males usually do not stay with the pride very long, and may even choose to live alone.

Lions will kill only when they are attacked or hungry. They are equipped to be excellent hunters. They have extremely powerful muscles. They can break another animal's neck with one blow of a paw. Or they tear the throat of a victim with their sharp, hooked claws or their sharp fangs.

Lions are *carnivorous*, or meat eaters. They feed on zebras, antelope, pigs, buffalo, and sometimes young elephants. Lions will eat as much meat as they can hold at a sitting.

Lions have always been admired for their strength and courage. Unfortunately, this admiration has led persons to hunt lions as a demonstration of their own strength and courage. Lions once roamed over much of the world, including Europe. But today they are mostly found in central and eastern Africa and western India. Lions live in open, grassy plains or woodland areas, not in deep forests or jungles. When not hunting, lions will lie peacefully in tall grass or shrubs. They will rarely attack people unless they are attacked first, or wounded. An enraged lion is a fierce fighter. Old or sick lions may attack for food but are more likely to hunt small, slow animals.

Today, most lions live in *game reserves* (national parks), where they are protected from hunters.

ALSO READ: CARNIVORE; CAT, WILD.

▲ *Carolus Linnaeus, the Swedish botanist who classified the plant kingdom. We still use a modified form of his system today.*

▼ *Lions hunt in groups, creeping silently through the long grass. It is usually the lionesses that do the actual killing. Sometimes, when other animals have made a kill, the lions will drive them off and eat the prey themselves.*

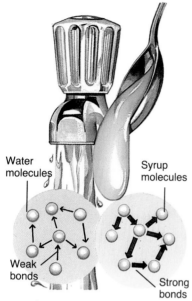

Water molecules

Syrup molecules

Weak bonds

Strong bonds

▲ *Some liquids flow faster than others; e.g., water flows faster than syrup. This is because the bonds between molecules of water are weaker than the bonds between molecules of syrup.*

LIQUID Everything in the world is a form of matter. Some matter is solid, such as the book you are holding. Some matter is gas, such as the air you are breathing. Some matter is liquid, such as water. All matter is made up of tiny particles called *molecules.*

In solids, the molecules are packed close together and fixed firmly in place. In liquids, the molecules are also packed close together, but they are not fixed firmly in place. They can move about freely. The molecules in gases are packed very loosely, and they can move about even more freely. The free movement of the molecules makes liquids and gases *fluid* (i.e., they flow).

Because a solid is not fluid, it keeps its shape. If you put a stone into a pitcher, the stone keeps its shape. If you pour water into the pitcher, the water spreads out and takes the shape of the pitcher. Gas likewise takes the shape of the container. Here is the one important difference between liquids and gases. The molecules in liquids tend to stay close together. This is called *cohesion.* But the molecules in gases tend to move away from each other. You can understand this fact by half-filling a bottle with water. The water takes on the shape of the bottle but it does not expand to fill the bottle. Any gas put into a container will expand to completely fill the container.

The molecules in a liquid are attracted to other substances. This is called *adhesion.* You get wet when you are in water because of adhesion. The molecules in the water are attracted to your skin.

■ **LEARN BY DOING**

The molecules of a liquid attract each other strongly enough to give its surface some strength. This attraction is called *surface tension.* You can show how surface tension works. Place a needle across the tines of a fork.

Slowly and gently lower the fork into a glass of water. The needle is made of steel, and so it should sink. But it floats, because the surface tension of the water holds it up. ■

A substance is called a liquid when it is a liquid at ordinary temperatures. Liquids become gases if they are heated to higher temperatures. Water heated to 212° F (100°C) becomes steam, a gas. Liquids cooled to lower temperatures become solids. Water cooled below 32° F (0°C) becomes ice, a solid. Air becomes a liquid if it is cooled to −312°F (−190°C). This temperature is very low: liquid air boils when it touches ice!

ALSO READ: CHEMISTRY, ELEMENT, GAS, MATTER, SOLID.

LIQUID CRYSTALS The display on a calculator or a digital watch has numbers that can change rapidly. This is because each figure or letter is made of a pattern of tiny stripes. Inside each stripe are some liquid crystals. Liquid crystals are substances in which the molecules twist when an electric current flows through them. This prevents light passing through the crystals and they appear to go black. As soon as the current stops, the molecules untwist and light passes again. When an electric current flows through one of the stripes on a digital display, the liquid crystals turn black. Electric signals go to the display from a microchip. The signals make some of the stripes turn black, and figures or letters appear. Liquid-crystal displays are ideal for watches and calculators because they use very little electric current. Heat, too, can affect liquid crystals, causing them to change color. Temperature indicators contain liquid crystals. They change color if something gets too hot or too cold.

ALSO READ: CHEMISTRY.

LISTER, JOSEPH (1827–1912)

Until the middle of the 19th century, almost half of the people who had open wounds or underwent surgery died of infection. A British surgeon, Joseph Lister, revolutionized surgical practice by introducing modern *antiseptic surgery*, or surgery without the risk of infection.

Joseph Lister was born at Upton, in the county of Essex, England. He was educated at University College, London. Later he held teaching posts at the University of Edinburgh and the University of Glasgow (both in Scotland).

Lister knew of the work of the French biochemist, Louis Pasteur, who had shown that infections are caused by the action of live bacteria. Lister experimented with various chemicals to find a way to kill bacteria. In 1868 he succeeded with a solution of carbolic acid.

He used this *antiseptic* (germ-killing) solution to clean wounds and *surgical incisions* (cuts made by a surgeon). He also used it to scrub his hands and arms thoroughly before operating. He even had the operating room sprayed with the carbolic acid solution. Surgical instruments were made bacteria-free by being heated to high temperatures.

Lister made other contributions to modern surgery, devising new operations and inventing several surgical instruments. He also introduced the use of *catgut*—strong thread made from sheep's intestines—for sewing surgical incisions.

ALSO READ: ANTIBIOTIC; MEDICINE; PASTEUR, LOUIS; SURGERY.

LISZT, FRANZ (1811–1886)

The Hungarian musician, Franz Liszt, is remembered today as a composer of music for the piano and orchestra. During his lifetime, he was best known as a pianist. His showmanship and dazzling playing made him a musical sensation in Europe.

Liszt was born in Raiding, Hungary. His parents recognized his musical talent when he was still a child. They took him to Vienna, Austria, when he was ten, for piano lessons. As a young man, he went on a nine-year concert tour of Europe and became internationally famous. After the tour, he devoted most of his time to teaching, composing, and conducting. He helped the great German composer, Richard Wagner, in his early career. Wagner later became Liszt's son-in-law.

Among Liszt's students were many who became great composers: Bizet, Saint-Saëns, Smetena, and Joseffy.

Much of Liszt's music is as brilliant and passionate as his piano playing must have been. In his *Hungarian Rhapsodies* for piano, he used the lilting and fiery music of the Hungarian gypsies. Liszt also wrote several popular symphonic tone poems—works for orchestra that tell a story or paint a picture with music. One of his most famous works of this kind is *Les Préludes*.

When he was 55, Liszt became a Roman Catholic abbé (priest), but he continued his musical work. He died in Bayreuth, Germany.

ALSO READ: COMPOSER, MUSIC, PIANO, ORCHESTRAS AND BANDS.

LITERACY

You can read these words and understand their meaning. You can write your name and, if you want, you can copy out this sentence or write one you made up yourself. You can read and write—you are *literate*. Literacy, which comes from the Latin for "letters of the alphabet," means the ability to read and write.

In the past, few people went to school, so few people learned how to read and write. It was not until the 1800's that governments began to realize it was worthwhile teaching ev-

▲ *Joseph Lister, the British surgeon who pioneered the use of antiseptics.*

As a boy Franz Liszt was delicate. Once when he was ill his father was so sure he would die that he ordered the local carpenter to make a coffin. In fact, Liszt lived to be almost 75.

▲ *Franz Liszt's appeal to musicians is a threefold one. He was a brilliant piano virtuoso, a teacher of other pianists, and a prolific composer.*

▲ *An illustrated page from* The Chronicles of France, England, and Spain, *written in the 1300's by the French historian Jean Froissart. Some of his stories were used in plays by William Shakespeare.*

▲ *An old illustration shows the shipwrecked sailor,* Robinson Crusoe. *Daniel Defoe's novel* Robinson Crusoe *(1719) was inspired by the real-life adventures of a Scottish sailor called Alexander Selkirk.*

eryone to be literate. Today, almost everyone in the United States learns to read and write at school. But some people have difficulty mastering literacy skills. They may need special help, even as adults.

In poor countries, where there are not enough schools or teachers, some children never get the chance to learn to read and write. But later, as adults, they may be able to attend classes as part of a literacy program.

Think what it would be like not to be able to enjoy reading a storybook, or look up facts in an encyclopedia, or find a friend's phone number in the telephone book. Truly, literacy is the key to knowledge.

LITERATURE   If you have ever cried at a movie or a play or laughed at a story, you already know some of the ways literature can make you feel. Literature is basically a communication in words of human thoughts and emotions. Before most people could read and write, literature consisted of stories and poems (often sung) that people made up and taught to their children and grandchildren. Stories and poems were remembered for many years, passing from generation to generation. Troubadours (traveling singers) made these stories and poems more widely known. But stories and poems that were written down could be copied and distributed to other towns and other countries. So writing came to be adopted as the best way for literature to reach a large number of people.

Purposes of Literature   One of the main purposes of literature is to help people understand human nature and experience. Another important goal of literature is to entertain people. You enjoy reading about other people and their experiences, and this reading often helps you understand more about people in general, or yourself in particular. Throughout the ages, peo-

ple have shared certain characteristics. They love, hate, admire, pity. They are amused, sad, afraid, cruel, and kind. Literature helps people to understand these emotions and their reasons for feeling them.

Literature appeals to the reader's emotions and imagination. Therefore, the writer chooses the words, phrases, and approach to the subject that will excite the reader's imagination. A writer chooses words for their sound and the thoughts people associate with them as well as for their specific meaning. For example, snow that is "white as white cow's milk" sounds somehow whiter and snowier than just "white snow." A writer's method of handling words, images (mental pictures), and sentences is called *style*. Every work of literature is a unique combination of content (subject matter), theme (the author's statement about human experience), and style.

Types of Literature   Literature that deals with imaginary people and situations is called *fiction*. Works of fic-

▼ *An engraving by Gustave Doré for the classic Spanish novel* Don Quixote *(1605–1615), by Miguel de Cervantes.*

tion are often realistic—that is, they seem as though they did or could happen. For example, Jane Austen's *Pride and Prejudice* (1813) takes place in an ordinary town. The parents, sisters, and friends of the main character are much like people all of us have met.

Many other fictional works are not realistic. They are based on imagination or fantasy. For example, we know that the events in Edgar Allan Poe's horror story, "The Tell-Tale Heart" (1843), could not take place, but they fascinate us anyhow. Such unrealistic stories are often given very realistic details to make the plot more believable. Fantasy fascinates you more if you are made to wonder if it actually *could* happen. Science fiction is a type of fantasy in which scientific details and ideas are used to make the fantasy more believable.

Essays (short compositions presenting the writer's personal views), biographies, and histories are *nonfiction* literature. James Boswell's biography of Samuel Johnson is nonfiction literature. Edward Gibbon's *The History of the Decline and Fall of the Roman Empire* (1776–1788) is also considered nonfiction literature.

The various forms of fictional literature differ in the kinds of plots and the number of characters on which they focus. A *short story* is a fictional work that (because of its shortness) usually has only one or two main characters and usually concentrates on one event in the main character's life. A *novel* is a longer work of fiction that may have many characters besides the *protagonist* (main character) and often covers several incidents over a long period of time in the characters' lives. A *narrative poem*, which tells a story in verse, also has a plot and characters. A *lyric poem* simply expresses in verse the poet's thoughts or emotions about a particular subject. A *dramatic poem* tells a story in verse through the dialogue (conversation) of the characters, just

▲ *An illustration by John Tenniel of the Mad Hatter's Tea Party for Lewis Carroll's famous story,* Alice's Adventures in Wonderland *(1865).*

as a prose (not written in verse) drama does. A drama, or play, is written to be acted on the stage. It usually has several main characters and usually focuses on one or two incidents in their lives. Everything that the audience knows about these characters depends on what they say and do. The playwright cannot tell you directly what a character thinks or feels.

Interpretation Not every reader will see the same theme, or meaning, in a work of literature. Everyone brings his or her own emotions and experiences to reading. Therefore, readers interpret works of literature in different ways. In fact, one of the things that makes good literature meaningful to people is that it can be interpreted and understood in several ways. For example, many people have enjoyed *Moby Dick* (1851), by Herman Melville, as an adventure story about Captain Ahab's search for the mighty white whale, Moby Dick. Many others see this novel as an essay about religion and the human soul. Both of these interpretations are true. Each results from a different view of the plot (series of events), characters, and theme of the novel. Sometimes a reader will interpret a book differently at different ages. For example, if you read *The Old Man and the Sea* (1952), by Ernest Hemingway, when

Some of the best-known children's books were originally written for adults. Perhaps the most notable are "Gulliver's Travels," "The Adventures of Huckleberry Finn," "The Pilgrim's Progress," "Robinson Crusoe," and the science fiction books of Jules Verne.

Dates	Author	Country	Work
about 1345–1400	Geoffrey Chaucer	England	Poetry
1564–1616	William Shakespeare	England	Plays, poetry
1771–1832	Sir Walter Scott	Scotland	Novels
1775–1817	Jane Austen	England	Novels
1803–1882	Ralph Waldo Emerson	U.S.A.	Essays, poetry
1809–1849	Edgar Allan Poe	U.S.A.	Stories, poetry
1812–1870	Charles Dickens	England	Novels
1819–1880	George Eliot (Mary Ann Evans)	England	Novels
1819–1891	Herman Melville	U.S.A.	Novels
1829–1910	Lev Tolstoy	Russia	Novels
1835–1910	Mark Twain (Samuel Clemens)	U.S.A.	Novels
1859–1930	Sir Arthur Conan Doyle	England	Novels, stories
1874–1963	Robert Frost	U.S.A.	Poetry
1878–1968	Upton Sinclair	U.S.A.	Novels
1885–1951	Sinclair Lewis	U.S.A.	Novels
1885–1930	D. H. Lawrence	England	Novels
1888–1953	Eugene O'Neill	U.S.A.	Novels, plays
1891–1976	Agatha Christie	England	Detective fiction
1892–1973	J(ohn) R(onald) R(eull) Tolkien	England	Fantasy Tales
1896–1970	John Dos Passos	U.S.A.	Novels
1897–1962	William Faulkner	U.S.A.	Novels
1898–1963	C(live) S(taples) Lewis	England	Poetry, novels
1899–1961	Ernest Hemingway	U.S.A.	Novels
1902–1968	John Steinbeck	U.S.A.	Novels
1915–	Arthur Miller	U.S.A.	Plays
1916–	Beverly Cleary	U.S.A.	Children's Novels
1917–1967	Carson McCullers	U.S.A.	Novels
1919–	J(erome) D(avid) Salinger	U.S.A.	Novels
1920–	Isaac Asimov	U.S.A.	Science fiction
1929–	Ursula K. LeGuin	U.S.A.	Novels
1930–	Ted Hughes	England	Poetry
1934–	Diana Wynne Jones	England	Children's Fantasy
1938–	Judy Blume	U.S.A.	Young Adult Novels

▲ *Mark Twain wrote stories about childhood in the rural United States.*

▲ *Sir Walter Scott wrote historical novels to get out of debt.*

▲ *Ralph Waldo Emerson was the United States's first great essayist.*

▲ *Charles Dickens's novels highlighted the squalor of his time.*

▲ *George Eliot (Mary Ann Evans), English author of* Middlemarch.

▲ *Edgar Allan Poe, American master of the horror story.*

▲ *John Steinbeck received the 1962 Nobel Prize for Literature.*

▲ *Beverly Cleary is a popular American author of children's fiction.*

▲ *Judy Blume's books recognize that children are real people.*

▲ *J.D. Salinger is best known for his novel* The Catcher in the Rye.

"Anne of Green Gables," by the Canadian writer Lucy M. Montgomery, is one of the most famous books in children's literature. Its heroine was described by Mark Twain as the most lovable child in fiction since Alice of "Alice in Wonderland."

▲ *Edna St. Vincent Millay was one of the best-loved U.S. poets of the 1920's and 1930's. Her verse is lyrical and easy to read.*

you are 12 and again when you are 20, you will "see" different meanings. The book is both an adventure story and a description of human courage and determination.

Themes in Literature The plot and characters in a piece of fiction work together to present the author's *theme*. Every writer has his or her own themes, and interpretations of them always differ. But the ideas that writers—and readers—are concerned with can be grouped into several *kinds* of themes. For example, people have been writing for centuries about such topics as love, death, religion, disappointment, hope—and writers today still have more to say about these subjects.

Writers and readers are always interested in what people learn about life as they grow up, since everyone has to go through this process. Mark Twain wrote *Huckleberry Finn* (1884), a novel about a boy who ran away from home and traveled down the Mississippi River on a raft with a runaway slave named Jim. From Jim and from the trip, Huck learned a great deal about independence and true friendship and about what he wanted out of life. Nearly 100 years later, J. D. Salinger wrote a novel, *The Catcher in the Rye* (1951), about another boy who was growing up. Holden, however, who had been put out of several schools, seemed to learn more about what he did *not* want in adult life than about what he wanted. In other novels, such as *The Heart Is a Lonely Hunter* (1940), by Carson McCullers, the main characters are introduced to the sadness—even tragedy—that people learn about when they grow up.

People have written on many other subjects, and there are many ways to interpret their writings. But as long as people share the same emotions and experiences, they will be interested in writing and reading literature. What subject do *you* like writing about?

Genres of Literature Some types of fiction are called *genres*. A genre is a type of literature that is different in some notable way from most of the other types of fiction being written. It is assumed that most readers will not be interested in genre fiction, but that those who do read it will be dedicated to it. You have probably read many books in each of the chief genres.

Probably the most important genre, in terms of literary value, is *science fiction* (SF). Most SF stories are about people, but people acting in situations that have never yet occurred. However, the writer gives a plausible explanation of how such situations could happen, usually using real or imagined science. Most SF stories are set in the future. You may have read some of the SF stories of the British writer H. G. Wells.

Fantasy is rather like SF, but fantasy writers usually do not give an explanation for the weird events in their stories. Perhaps you have read some of the fantasies of J. R. R. Tolkien or of Alan Garner. *Horror fantasy* is a type of fantasy that tries to scare you. Ask an adult to look through a horror novel before you read it yourself. Some horror writers, such as Stephen King, write so well that their books can give you nightmares!

Crime fiction is of two main types. In one, detective fiction, all that really matters is the plot. This involves a mysterious crime (almost always a murder), and the solving of the crime by a detective. Some famous detectives in fiction are Ellery Queen, Hercule Poirot, Gideon Fell, Philip Marlowe, and of course Sherlock Holmes.

The other type of crime fiction deals with the *psychology* (mental make-up) of people who either commit or are the victims of criminal acts. Stories of this type often have detectives, just like detective fiction. Sometimes the heroes of these stories are spies—like James Bond.

Other genres include *romance novels* and *Westerns*. Romances tell about how two people meet and fall in love. Usually there are lots of difficulties before they can marry each other. One romance novelist, Kathleen Lindsay, wrote more than 900 books! Westerns are set in the Wild West, with cowboys fighting either each other or Indians. Perhaps you have read Westerns by Zane Grey or Louis L'Amour.

How many books do *you* own that are genre books? If you look at your books you will find that many of them are in one or another of the genres listed here. You may find that very few of them are *not* genre books. The genres of literature are, today, producing some very exciting writing.

Literary Awards A literary award is a prize given for an outstanding work, or group of works, of writing. Each year, all over the world, many literary awards are presented for novels, biographies, histories, drama, poetry, and other kinds of writing.

Perhaps the most respected literary award is the *Nobel Prize for Literature.* Writers from anywhere may be chosen for this award. The prize is presented at a ceremony in Stockholm, Sweden, each year. Nine U.S. writers have won the Nobel Prize for Literature—Sinclair Lewis (1930), Eugene O'Neill (1936), Pearl Buck (1938), William Faulkner (1949), Ernest Hemingway (1954), John Steinbeck (1962), Saul Bellow (1976), Isaac Bashevis Singer (1978), and Czeslaw Milosz (1980).

Among nearly 100 literary awards presented each year in the United States are the *Pulitzer Prizes,* established in 1917 by the newspaper publisher, Joseph Pulitzer. These are given for journalistic achievements and to the writers of works chosen as the best U.S. novel, play, history, biography, and poetry. Robert Frost won the prize four times for his poetry. John F. Kennedy won it in 1957 for his biographical work, *Profiles in Courage.*

Another important group of U.S. literary awards are the *American Book Awards,* given each year by a committee representing the book-publishing industry. These awards are presented in important fields of literature.

Many awards are given in the United States for outstanding children's books. Among the best known are the *Newbery Medal,* the *Laura Ingalls Wilder Medal,* the *Jane Addams Children's Book Award,* and the *Boston Globe-Horn Book Awards.* The American Library Association chooses the winners of the Newbery (for best-written children's book) and the *Caldecott* (for best-illustrated children's book) awards. The *Regina Medal* (for continued contribution to children's literature) is awarded each year by the Catholic Library Association. In some states, such as Vermont and Oklahoma, awards are given for books judged by children themselves. In Canada, the Canadian Library Association chooses the book of the year for children, a top award.

Many literary awards are given by organizations for books written about the topic in which the organization is interested. These include books about certain regions of the United States, certain historical periods, and religions. For example, the *B'nai B'rith Award* is presented for the best

▲ *William Faulkner, U.S. novelist and one of the great figures of literature in the first half of this century. He wrote about modern life in the South. In 1949 he received the Nobel Prize for Literature.*

◄ *Nobel Literature Prize-winner Pearl S. Buck receives her award from King Gustav V of Sweden on December 10, 1938.*

Perhaps the best-loved children's book by an American author is "Little Women," by Louisa May Alcott. The book tells of the experiences of Jo March and her sisters, but the story is the real-life one of the Alcott family. Jo March is Louisa herself.

▲ *A view of Kaunas, a city in central Lithuania, located on the Neman River.*

book on Jewish life or Judaism, and the *National Catholic Book Awards* are given for special achievements in Catholic book publishing. The *Bancroft Prizes* are presented by Columbia University for books on U.S. history, diplomacy, and international relations.

Among the most outstanding foreign book awards are the *Canadian Governor General's Literary Awards*, the United Kingdom's *Booker Prize*, and France's *Prix Goncourt* and *Grand Prix du Roman*.

Literary awards take many different forms. Some are silver cups, silver and gold medals, and money in varying amounts. Organizations often give their awards in the form of fellowships and grants to help writers further their studies and careers. Often there is no money involved, just honor. Each year the Western Writers of America honor the author of the best piece of writing about the West. Another award is the "Edgar," given by the Mystery Writers of America for the best mystery novel. Science fiction has two major awards presented annually, the "Hugo" and the "Nebula." Both are awarded in various categories, such as short story, novel, and novelette (short novel).

We read literature for many reasons, and the reasons may change as we grow older. But most people read because reading is one of life's great pleasures.

For further information on:
Kinds of Literature, *see* AUTOBIOGRAPHY, BIOGRAPHY, DIARY, DRAMA, FOLKLORE, LEGEND, NOVEL, POETRY, SCIENCE FICTION, SHORT STORY.
Literary Awards, *see* CALDECOTT AWARD, NEWBERY MEDAL, NOBEL PRIZE.
Related Topics, *see* BOOK, CHILDREN'S LITERATURE, GREEK LITERATURE, LANGUAGE ARTS, LANGUAGES, LIBRARY, PHILOSOPHY, PRINTING, RENAISSANCE, WRITTEN LANGUAGE.
For individual authors, poets, and playwrights, see Index.

LITHUANIA   The Lithuanian Soviet Socialist Republic is a flat land covered with forests, streams, meadows, marshes, and hundreds of small lakes. It is bordered by Latvia on the north, Russia and Poland on the east and south, and the Baltic Sea on the west. The country has long, cold winters and short, warm summers. The capital is Vilna (Vilnius). (See the map with the article on EUROPE.)

Approximately half the land in Lithuania is suitable for farming. Many of the people earn their living in agriculture. Much of the agricultural work is done on collective farms, where each family works its own land, but the products are sold together, and the profits are divided. Other Lithuanians work in manufacturing. Many people who live along the Baltic Sea coast earn their living by fishing. By the 1300's, Lithuanian rulers had built an empire that stretched from the Baltic Sea to the Black Sea. In 1386, Lithuania and Poland were united under a Lithuanian Grand Duke, Jagiello, who became Wladyslaw II when he married the Queen of Poland. Later, Poland and Russia ruled the land. In 1918, Lithuania regained its independence, and the people elected a democratic government. Lithuania was free only until 1939, when Russian soldiers crossed the border. A Communist government came to power in 1940, and the country became part of the Soviet Union. During World War II, the Germans occupied Lithuania, and the country suffered much hardship. Almost all Lithuanian Jews were killed by the Germans.

Lithuania, along with Estonia and Latvia, became part of the Soviet Union again after the war. For years many Lithuanians fought a guerrilla war against their Soviet occupiers. Some fled to other countries. Thousands were sent to labor camps in Siberia. Many Russians then came to live in Lithuania. As a result, about half of the people now living in Lithuania do not speak Lithuanian. In 1990, Lithuania declared it would become independent of the U.S.S.R., but the Soviet government said "No."

ALSO READ: BALTIC SEA, ESTONIA, LATVIA, SOVIET UNION.

LITTLE LEAGUE BASEBALL

The main difference between regular baseball and Little League baseball is size. The players in Little League baseball are smaller, the playing field is smaller, and so are the ball and bat. Instead of nine innings, a Little League game has six.

The game is designed to teach young boys and girls the basic rules of baseball, and to give them a chance to play the game. The first Little League was formed in Williamsport, Pennsylvania, in 1939. Since then, the game has spread throughout the United States and to many other countries. Over two million boys and girls play in 10,000 Little Leagues around the world. The best teams attend the world series play-offs in Williamsport each year. The winning team at the series becomes the Little League champion of the world for that year.

Little League baseball is for boys and girls between the ages of 8 and 12. Each team consists of 12 to 15 members. Many teams are named for professional baseball teams, such as the Orioles, Yankees, and Dodgers.

Little League baseball sponsors a Senior League for players 13 to 15 years old and a Big League for those 16 to 18. The Senior League plays a world series in Gary, Indiana, and the Big League has one in Fort Lauderdale, Florida.

Almost every community has at least one Little League team. If you want to join a team, ask your physical education teacher or the athletic director of your school.

ALSO READ: BASEBALL.

▲ *The batter gets ready to hit the ball in a game of Little League Baseball.*

LIVER The liver is the largest gland and one of the largest organs in the human body. It is soft and flat in shape, a dark reddish or chocolate brown in color, and in an adult weighs 3 to 4 pounds (1.4–1.8 kg). It is located in the right side of the abdomen, just below the stomach. It is divided into four *lobes*, or sections.

The liver is one of the most important organs in the body. If the liver is damaged so that it cannot perform its work, the body cannot continue to function, and death will occur. The liver produces *bile*, a liquid substance needed for digesting fats. The bile is stored in a small sac called the *gall bladder*. Bile empties into the small intestine from the gall bladder by means of a bile duct.

Glycogen is stored by the liver. Blood travels from the small intestine to the liver, carrying a sugar, called *glucose*. The liver changes glucose into glycogen and stores it. When the body needs extra energy, the liver

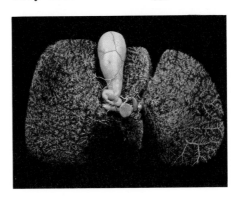

◀ *A model of the liver, showing the countless blood vessels. The liver is the body's "chemical factory." The* gall bladder, *shown yellow, stores* bile. *The red artery (center) and dark blue veins are those of the liver's normal blood supply. The* hepatic artery (*pale blue, center*) *carries food from the digestive system.*

rapidly changes the glycogen back into glucose sugar. The glucose then travels through the bloodstream, providing energy for the body cells.

Certain poisonous waste products are produced by body cells as they do their work. The liver combines these substances with other chemicals to make nonpoisonous ones. The wastes are then processed by the kidneys and excreted.

The liver also stores vitamins. Vitamins A and D and the various B vitamins are held in the liver for the body to use when necessary. Copper and iron are also stored.

The liver also can make various substances. Two, *fibrinogen* and *prothrombin*, help the blood to clot to stop bleeding. Another product of the liver is *albumin*. This helps the blood pass through the capillary walls.

The liver may be badly damaged by diseases such as malaria, hepatitis, and dysentery. If these diseases are cured, the liver can go on with its work. If they are not, the liver cannot get rid of the bile that it makes. Bile then goes into the blood, causing the skin to turn yellow—the color of the bile. This condition is called *jaundice*.

People who drink too much alcohol for a long time may develop a disease of the liver named *cirrhosis*.

ALSO READ: BLOOD, CIRCULATORY SYSTEM, DIGESTION, DISEASE, GLAND, HUMAN BODY, VITAMINS AND MINERALS.

LIVINGSTONE, DAVID (1813–1873) Many people remember the name of the Scottish missionary and explorer, David Livingstone, from the words, "Dr. Livingstone, I presume?" This formal greeting was spoken in 1872 by the Welsh-born journalist and explorer, Henry Morton Stanley. For eight months, Stanley had been searching for Livingstone in the jungles of central Africa. When he entered Livingstone's camp, he spoke those famous words.

David Livingstone was born in Blantyre, Scotland. He first traveled to Africa in 1841, hoping to convert the African people to Christianity. On his travels to distant villages, he began to explore unknown sections of Africa. He was the first European to see the mighty Victoria Falls, located on the border of Zimbabwe and Zambia. *Missionary Travels and Researches in South Africa*, published in 1857, made him famous. In 1866, Livingstone set out to discover the source of the great Nile River. He journeyed deep into central Africa, but he was too far south to find the Nile. He did succeed in finding a source of the Congo River.

During his explorations, Livingstone was horrified to see the terrible effects the slave trade was having on the people of Africa. His reports of what he saw, published in 1865, helped to bring about an end to slave-buying and selling. During his long, hard travels, he became dangerously ill. For more than two years, nothing was heard about him. The *New York Herald* newspaper sent Stanley to Africa to find Livingstone. After their famous meeting, the two men explored the region around Lake Tanganyika in what is now Zaire. Livingstone refused to leave Africa, where he later died in the village of a tribal chieftain.

ALSO READ: EXPLORATION; SLAVERY; STANLEY, HENRY MORTON.

▼ *David Livingstone, the Scottish missionary, arrives at Lake Ngami, in what is now Botswana, in 1849.*

LIZARD Have you ever seen an animal drop its tail off? Or squirt blood out of its eyelids? Some kinds of lizards can do such things in order to defend themselves.

Lizards are a group (over 3,000 species) of reptiles closely related to snakes. Lizards have dry, scaly skin, which they shed periodically. Most species have four legs, although some have no legs and are often confused with snakes. (The glass snake is actually not a snake but a legless lizard.) Nearly all lizards have tails that are much longer than their bodies, although the horned toad (actually a lizard) has a rather short tail. Lizards may vary in length from a few inches (geckos and chameleons) to several feet (Komodo dragons). Most lizards are less than two feet (61 cm) long.

Lizards can be almost any color or combination of colors. The male often has brightly colored patches. Some types of lizards, such as chameleons, can change color to match their backgrounds so they are hard to see. Light and temperature influence a lizard's color. The male lizard's color also changes during a fight with another lizard.

Lizards live in nearly all parts of the world, but they are most common in warm and tropical regions. Like all reptiles, lizards are cold-blooded, which means that their body temperature varies with the temperature of their surroundings. Because of this, desert lizards often must hide in the shade or burrow into the sand when the sun becomes too hot or the night too cold.

Lizards have adapted their methods of movement to their environments. Desert lizards have sharp claws on their feet that enable them to dig into sand rapidly. One type of lizard, the gecko, can walk on walls and ceilings because it has pads on its toes that are made of small, hooked growths. These pads enable the gecko to cling to surfaces that look smooth. One variety of agamid lizard can "fly" (glide, really) from tree to tree. By moving several of its long ribs, which are connected to a *membrane* (flap of skin), a small "sail" is formed. The lizard uses this sail to glide for short distances. Legless lizards move by wriggling.

Since most species of lizards are harmless, they have developed ways of scaring off attackers. When a certain type of lizard disconnects its tail from its body, the tail continues to twitch. As the attacker watches—or eats—the tail, the lizard escapes. The lizard then grows a new tail. The

▲ *Some lizards may look a little scary, but almost all are harmless. The humble green lizard is found in many areas.*

The world's largest lizard is the Komodo dragon. The biggest specimen measured spanned more than 10 feet (3 m) and weighed twice as much as an average man. Komodo dragons live on a few small Indonesian islands, where they kill and eat goats and small deer.

▼ *The Gila monster, one of only two poisonous lizards, lives in American deserts, wide canyons, and washes in rocky areas. Its bite can kill.*

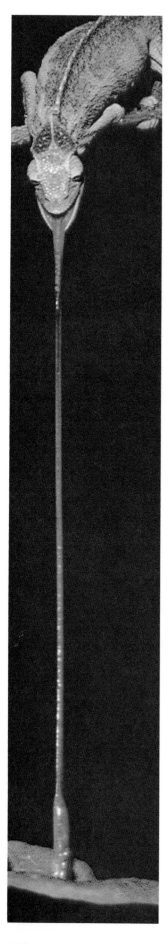

horned toad squirts a little blood out of its eyelids to drive away its attacker. The frilled lizard has a wide membrane around its neck that it can spread out like a ruffle to make itself look bigger, and so frighten away an enemy.

Many species are carnivorous (meat-eating); others are herbivorous (plant-eating). Some types are omnivorous (eat both plants and animals). In some areas, lizards are valuable to farmers because they eat troublesome pests, such as insects.

Some types of female lizards are *oviparous*, which means that they lay eggs. Other species are *ovoviviparous*, which means that the eggs are warmed inside the mother's body and the young are born alive.

Geckos and the smooth, shiny skinks live in North America and other parts of the world. Iguanas are also found in the Western Hemisphere. The American chameleon is actually one kind of iguana. The only poisonous lizards in North America are Gila monsters and beaded lizards, found in the southwestern United States and in Mexico.

ALSO READ: ALLIGATORS AND CROCODILES, REPTILE, SNAKE.

LLAMA see CAMEL.

LOCAL GOVERNMENT Have you ever looked at the words printed on the truck collecting garbage near your home? Do they say something like "City of Chicago," "Arlington County," or "Town of Stuntz"? Who is in charge of sanitation where you live? Your local government. Who is in charge of the water supply, the police and fire departments, or the

◀ *The chameleon can change color to disguise itself. In some species, the tongue is longer than the body, and the eyes can move independently of each other!*

▲ *Local governments are responsible for many important services. One is to provide an efficient and effective fire department for the community.*

traffic signs and signals where you live? These activities and responsibilities are usually also handled by local governments.

The U.S. Constitution states exactly what the Federal Government (which governs the entire nation) may or may not do. Any power not given to the Federal Government is handled by the state governments. State governments have their own state constitutions, which describe the state's powers and tell what powers local governments may have. Each state constitution is different, so the local governments in each state vary.

Forms of Local Government The area under the control of a local government may be established in several ways. It may be based on population, land area, or simply on the nature of a region. There are three main forms of local government in the United States—town, municipal, and county.

TOWN GOVERNMENT. In the New England states, the *town* is the main unit of local government. Voters gather in town meetings to vote on the town's budget, to vote on special expenditures, to pass local laws, and discuss other local government affairs.

MUNICIPAL GOVERNMENT. Many people throughout the United States live in urban (city) areas, such as New York City, Chicago, and Los Angeles. Most cities operate under a *municipal* form of government. The governing body of a municipality is usually an elected council, which is sometimes composed of an upper and a lower chamber, or house. The chief officer is an elected mayor. Some municipalities have a city manager. A city manager is a nonelective official hired by the council to manage the affairs of the city and to appoint and supervise the heads of the various departments.

COUNTY GOVERNMENT. The *county* is the main unit of local government in most of the United States. The people elect representatives, usually called the County Board, to impose taxes, supervise county officials, and perform certain administrative functions. These functions may include the management of the school system, fire department, water system, and other local departments. The County Board may also make local laws and set up local courts.

Responsibilities Many of the duties and much of the power of local governments are connected in some way with the state and federal governments. State authorities supervise many activities of local governments, especially those affecting public institutions, such as public schools, hospitals, prisons, and boards of health. The local courts are administered by the local, state, or federal government, depending on the kinds of legal cases they handle. Decisions of judges in local courts may be overruled by judges in state and federal courts. State and federal government authorities may also help supervise the many local institutions and projects to which they have given financial aid. The local government usually has total or nearly total authority over the police department, fire department,

sanitation department, water- and air-pollution control, and the transportation system. The local government also provides housing and food for the poor. It keeps records of births, marriages, deaths, and house and land sales; collects taxes; and runs elections.

ALSO READ: CITY, COMMUNITY, COUNTY, COURT SYSTEM, GOVERNMENT, STATES' RIGHTS, SUBURB.

LOCKS AND KEYS A lock is a mechanical device used to fasten doors, chests, and lids. Most locks consist of a bolt with a guard that can be released by a key. Locks were invented by the Chinese 4,000 years ago. An ancient Egyptian lock from about 2000 B.C., found with its key in the ruins of a city, was made of wood. The Greeks and Romans used locks of simple design and made large keys of iron or bronze. Skilled craftworkers in the 1500's designed beautifully carved locks and keys.

The simplest form of lock is a *ward lock*, or a *fixed lock*. It has a bolt that is moved backward or forward by a key. The *tumbler* or *lever lock* contains metal pieces of various heights known as tumblers, or levers. These keep the bolt from being moved until the tumblers are released by a key of the correct shape.

The *pin-tumbler cylinder lock* or *Yale lock* was invented and patented by Linus Yale, Jr., in the early 1860's. It was the first lock to use a small, flat key in place of a large one.

Some day you will need a combination lock for your school locker. Combination locks are worked by dials that are turned certain distances back and forth to release the tumblers inside. There are numbers around the dial to show you where to stop on each turn. Most locks of this kind have between 100,000 and 1,000,000 possible combinations, so they are very secure.

▼ *A lever-tumbler lock contains a set of levers that hold the bolt closed or open. Springs keep the levers in position so that the bolt cannot move. When the key is turned, the levers are raised and line up to free the bolt. The key moves the bolt in or out to unlock or lock the door.*

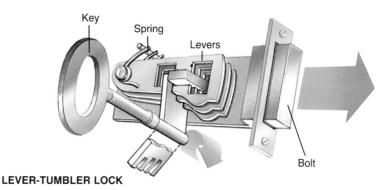

Key
Spring
Levers
Bolt

LEVER-TUMBLER LOCK

LOCOMOTIVE

▶ *The modern cylinder (Yale) lock has a cylinder block and an inner tumbler. Springs in the block push pins of different lengths into tubes in the tumbler. These pins are supported by the tumbler's internal pins, which are also of different lengths. The lock is closed, because the tumbler cannot turn (1). When a key of the correct pattern is inserted (2), its "bumps" raise the pins to just the right height to allow the tumbler to turn as the key is turned (3).*

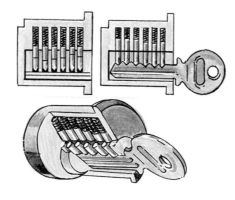

London is very slowly sinking into its foundations and the level of the Thames River is slowly rising. As a result, extra-high tides could flood much of London. To prevent this happening, a great barrier has been built across the Thames at Woolwich. If very high tides happen, the barrier can be raised and London will be safe.

▼ *A view of London in 1749. London's river frontage, dominated by St. Paul's Cathedral with its famous dome, was renowned as one of the most beautiful in Europe.*

It is made up of a revolving cylinder or plug. Five or six pin tumblers fall down into the cylinder when it is locked. The key must raise all five pins, which have different lengths, before the lock will open. The most common form of cylinder lock used in the home is the *night latch*, operated by a key from the outside and a knob from the inside. When the pin tumblers are inside the lock itself, as in a *padlock*, it is called a *pin-tumbler lock*.

The *dial* or *combination lock*, designed for safes and bank vaults, is not operated by a key. Turning a dial in the right sequence of numbers arranges a set of tumblers or wheels so that a bolt is released. Combination locks can have many possible combinations. A *time lock* can be opened only at a certain hour, when a clock releases the bolt.

A series of locks can be made so that a *master key* or *skeleton key* will open any of the locks. Each of these locks also has its own key that can open only that lock.

LOCOMOTIVE see RAILROAD.

LOGIC see REASONING.

LONDON London is the capital of the United Kingdom. It is one of the largest cities in the world, with a population of about 6,678,000. London is a bustling seaport and world trade and financial center full of warehouses, offices, homes, and markets. But in this modern city are many beautiful historic buildings. The ancient ceremony of the changing of the guard can be seen at Buckingham Palace, the official home of the monarch. The guards wear colorful uniforms and tall black hats called "bearskins." The person called "Lord Mayor of London" is an honorary official.

London is built near the mouth of the River Thames. In A.D. 43, some decades after the Romans arrived in Britain, they built a bridge over the Thames. This was guarded by a walled town, which the Romans called Londinium.

When the Roman Empire collapsed, the barbaric tribes who invaded England had little use for cities. London lay deserted for about 300 years. Alfred the Great, king of the West Saxons, occupied the town in the late A.D. 800's. He rebuilt the Roman walls and made London a center for business and trade.

When the Normans from France conquered England in A.D. 1066, London was a busy city. The Norman leader, William the Conqueror, had a fortress built to guard London Bridge. This became the Tower of London, used for centuries as a royal palace and prison.

Most of the buildings in Old London were made of wood, with thatch (straw) roofs. In 1666, the Great Fire of London burned for five days and destroyed most of the city. A brilliant English architect, Sir Christopher Wren, helped plan the city's rebuilding. Stone and brick were used for the houses. Many beautiful churches, including Saint Paul's Cathedral, were built. Over the centuries, London spread far beyond the old city walls. Tree-lined avenues, squares, and spacious parks were made.

London was badly bombed during World War II, but most of the historic buildings were saved. The Tower of London is now a national monument and museum where the Crown Jewels are kept. The Houses of Parliament are easily recognized by the tower of the huge clock, whose bell is known as Big Ben. Nearby is Westminster Abbey, where the kings and queens of England have been crowned since the days of William the Conqueror. The prime minister of Britain lives in a house at 10 Downing Street.

Londoners have parks and gardens to enjoy. Some of the largest are Hyde Park, Kensington Gardens, and Regent's Park, which has a zoo. London is a center for opera houses, concert halls, theaters, art galleries and museums, including the British Museum.

ALSO READ: ALFRED THE GREAT, BIG BEN, CROWN JEWELS, ENGLISH HISTORY, THAMES RIVER, TOWER OF LONDON, WESTMINSTER ABBEY.

▲ *The Houses of Parliament, beside the Thames River in London, the capital of the United Kingdom. The two chambers of the British Parliament meet here.*

LONDON, JACK (1876–1916)
Some of the most popular adventure stories in U.S. literature were written by Jack London. He was born in San Francisco, California. He went to sea at 15 and saw much of the world. Among many adventures, he searched for gold in the Klondike (a part of Canada's Yukon Territory). His first published book was *The Son of the Wolf*, a collection of short stories about his gold-rush days.

Probably his most widely read work is *The Call of the Wild*. It tells about a tame dog who is stolen from his California home and taken to the Yukon. In the end, he becomes leader of a wolf pack. In *White Fang*, Jack London tells how a wolf is turned into a pet.

In *Martin Eden*, London tells the story of a poor, young seaman who works hard to become a writer. In this book, London is really writing much about his own life. *The Iron Heel* gives a powerful vision of life in a fascist state. This book reflects London's lifelong support for socialism.

ALSO READ: LITERATURE, NOVEL.

Somewhere beneath London is a huge lake, thought by geologists to be part of a subterranean lake that stretches all the way beneath France.

▲ *Jack London, the U.S. novelist. He is most famous for his animal stories, but he wrote also some important novels about society as he saw it.*

▲ *Henry Wadsworth Longfellow, the U.S. poet best known for his "Song of Hiawatha" and "Paul Revere's Ride."*

▼ *Cinderella's Castle in Disneyland, Anaheim, near Los Angeles. Disneyland is a playground for both young and old.*

LONGFELLOW, HENRY WADSWORTH (1807–1882) Henry Wadsworth Longfellow was the United States's most popular poet during much of the 1800's. He wrote "The Village Blacksmith," "Paul Revere's Ride," and "The Children's Hour," three poems that remain well known. He also composed the beautifully flowing story-poem, *The Song of Hiawatha*, based on authentic legends of the North American Indians. It has been estimated that *The Song of Hiawatha* sold about a million copies during Longfellow's lifetime, probably a world record for a book of poetry. One of the most famous passages from this poem describes the home of Nokomis and her son, Hiawatha: By the shores of Gitche Gumee,

By the shining Big-Sea-Water,
Stood the wigwam of Nokomis,
Daughter of the Moon, Nokomis.
The Courtship of Miles Standish, "The Wreck of the Hesperus," and *Evangeline*, which are all based on North American legends, are other well-known poems by Longfellow.

Longfellow was born in Portland, Maine. He attended Bowdoin College in Maine, and studied at several universities in Europe. Before becoming a writer, he taught modern languages at Bowdoin and later at Harvard University.

One of Longfellow's most interesting collections of poems is *Tales of a Wayside Inn*, stories in verse told by travelers staying at a real inn located in Sudbury, Massachusetts. The Wayside Inn, the oldest operating inn in the United States, is now visited by thousands of people every year. Longfellow's house in Cambridge, Massachusetts, is also a popular attraction for tourists. When Longfellow died, a statue of him was placed in the Poet's Corner of Westminster Abbey in London. He was the first United States poet to be honored in this famous resting place.

LONG ISLAND see NEW YORK, NEW YORK CITY.

LOS ANGELES The city of Los Angeles, California, has been one of the fastest-growing in the United States during this century. In 1900, its population was a little over 100,000. Today, Los Angeles has more than three million people, making it the third largest city in the nation. Its metropolitan area, with about eight million people, ranks second only to that of New York City. Los Angeles covers about 460 square miles (1,200 sq. km). It completely surrounds several independent cities, such as Beverly Hills and San Fernando. The city is one of the major commercial and industrial centers in the United States. Hollywood, a part of Greater Los Angeles, has been famous as a movie-making center since the early 20th century, and is today the nation's most important center for the making of films for television.

In 1781, a Spanish missionary, Father Junipero Serra, and the governor of the Mexican province of Alta California, Don Felipe de Neve, founded a town called (in English) "The Town of Our Lady, the Queen of the Angels, of Porciúncula." A few settlers lived around a *plaza* (town square) by the Porciúncula River. The old plaza is now a park in downtown Los Angeles.

In 1846, Los Angeles was captured by the United States in the Mexican War. It soon became a thriving frontier town. After the discovery of gold in California in 1849, Los Angeles served as a source of food for the booming mining towns in the north. The name was shortened to Los Angeles as the region grew.

A transcontinental railroad, completed in 1876, connected Los Angeles with the East and brought in many new settlers.

Oil was discovered in the city of Los Angeles and under the waters of San Pedro Bay. Oil wells began pumping inside the city limits in the 1920's. From 1900 to 1920, the vast growth of all the industries in Los Angeles caused the population to triple—from 100,000 to more than 300,000 people! During World War II, the aircraft and other war industries expanded greatly, bringing hundreds of thousands of people to Los Angeles.

Many people come to Los Angeles because of its beautiful climate and scenery. The rapid growth of the city has, unfortunately, brought many problems. There are too few buses in this sprawling city, and no subway. The many expressways, called *freeways*, through and around the city have created a traffic problem and increased air pollution. The *smog* of Los Angeles has become a dangerous health hazard, and no solution to the problem has yet been found.

The city has an area of 465 square miles (1,204 sq. km). It has 11 universities and colleges, 1,642 public schools, 800 private schools, and 61 public libraries.

Los Angeles lives under the constant threat of earthquakes. Major earthquakes are rare, but slight tremors, landslides, and mudflows cause thousands of dollars' worth of damage each year. One earthquake, however, in 1971 killed 65 persons and caused $1 billion in damage.

ALSO READ: AIR POLLUTION, CALIFORNIA, EARTHQUAKE, MEXICAN WAR, MEXICO, WESTWARD MOVEMENT.

LOUIS, KINGS OF FRANCE

France has been ruled by 18 kings with the name of Louis.

Louis I (778–840) succeeded his father Charlemagne as king of the Franks and emperor of the Romans, in 814. Louis divided his lands among his four sons, who fought each other

bitterly and rebelled against their father. Louis I supported the Catholic Church in France, and was called "The Pious."

Louis II (846–879) was called "The Stammerer." He succeeded his father Charles II as king of France in 877, and had a short reign.

Louis III (about 863–882) was the son of Louis II. He became joint ruler of France with his brother Carloman in 879.

Louis IV (921–954) was the son of King Charles III and grandson of Louis II. By this time, France was split up into many regions, each ruled by a noble. No king since the days of Charlemagne had been strong enough to control all of France, and the nobles were often more powerful than the king. Louis's father was overthrown by the nobles, and Louis spent much of his childhood in England. In 936, several of the nobles asked Louis to return, and he was crowned king of France.

Louis V (about 967–987) was known as "The Sluggard" (lazy person). He succeeded his father King Lothair as king in 986. Louis V was the last king of the Carolingian dynasty (ruling family), founded by Charlemagne. When Louis died, the French people rejected his son and

▲ *Downtown Los Angeles. The people depend almost entirely on their cars and the expansive freeway system to travel about.*

▲ *Louis IX (Saint Louis) ruled France from 1226 until 1270. In the Middle Ages he was regarded as the model of what a Christian king should be.*

▲ *Louis XI, French king from 1461 to 1483. He was harsh, but made many wise reforms.*

▲ *Louis XIV, the "Sun King," who ruled France from 1643 to 1715.*

▼ *Louis XVI, French king from 1774 to 1792, ended his life on the guillotine in 1793.*

chose Hugh Capet of a popular noble family as king of France.

Louis VI (about 1080–1137) succeeded his father King Philip I in 1108. Louis was a gluttonous eater who became known as "The Fat."

Louis VII (about 1121–1180) succeeded his father, Louis VI, in 1137. In 1147, he led the second of the great Crusades, or Christian military campaigns, against the Muslims in the Holy Land. Louis divorced his wife, Queen Eleanor of Aquitaine, in 1152. Eleanor then married King Henry II of England, to whom she brought the large French region of Aquitaine. The English possession of Aquitaine led to quarrels between the two countries and was one of the main causes of the Hundred Years' War (1337–1453).

Louis VIII (1187–1226) was the son of King Philip Augustus of France and grandson of Louis VII. Before Louis became king, several rebellious English nobles asked him for help against their unpopular king, John. Louis invaded England with an army, but was defeated. Louis became king of France in 1223, but he died three years later.

Louis IX (1214–1270), or Saint Louis, succeeded his father, Louis VIII, in 1226, when he was 12 years old. His mother, Queen Blanche, acted as regent until Louis was old enough to rule. The young king was just and fair to nobles and peasants

alike, and greatly loved by the people. King Henry III of England made war on France, trying to increase his territories there. Louis defeated him in 1242, but generously allowed him to keep almost all of his existing land. Louis hoped that by doing this he would remove the possible cause of more wars. Louis also led two crusades to the Holy Land. He died of the plague in northern Africa while on the Eighth Crusade. In 1297, Louis was declared a saint.

Louis X (1289–1316) was known as "The Quarreler." He succeeded his father, King Philip IV of France, in 1314. During his reign, the nobles began to regain power.

Louis XI (1423–1483) was a cunning man, who became known as "The Spider." His father was King Charles VII. When Louis became king of France in 1461, he forced the rich to pay huge taxes. But he also defeated the most powerful of the nobles, united France, built a strong army, and encouraged the work of the townspeople. He was a great patron of the arts and sciences.

Louis XII (1462–1515), son of Charles, Duke of Orléans, became king of France in 1498, after the death of his cousin Charles VIII, who left no heirs. Louis worked to improve the living conditions of the French, especially the peasants. He became known as the "Father of the People."

Louis XIII (1601–1643) was only nine years old when he became king. His father, King Henry IV, was assassinated in 1610. Louis had poor health and never had the strength to rule alone. His mother, Marie de' Médici, first acted as regent. Later, Louis's brilliant chief minister, Cardinal Richelieu, governed France.

Louis XIV (1638–1715) succeeded his father, Louis XIII, as king of France in 1643. He was only five years old, and his mother, Queen Anne, became regent. During Louis's childhood, France was governed by

the chief minister, Cardinal Mazarin. After Mazarin died in 1661, the king took control of the government and eventually became known as the "Grand Monarch." The sun became the symbol of his power, and he is often known as the "Sun King." He built a magnificent palace at Versailles, outside Paris. During Louis' reign the arts flourished. Louis led France into four wars with other European countries. But he was defeated, and by the end of the wars, much of France's wealth had been used up.

Louis XV (1710–1774) was the great-grandson of Louis XIV. He succeeded Louis XIV as king of France in 1715, when he was five years old. France was ruled by a regent, the Duke of Orléans, until 1723. Louis was then guided by his capable chief minister, Cardinal Fleury. After Fleury's death, Louis devoted most of his time to the pleasures of court life. He waged two expensive and unsuccessful wars, which the French peasants were forced to pay for with huge taxes. But Louis showed very little concern for their unhappiness.

Louis XV's reign did much to bring on the French Revolution. During his reign France lost its colonies in Canada and India.

Louis XVI (1754–1793) succeeded his grandfather Louis XV in 1774. His great passion was hunting, and he left governing to his ministers. The French people were now demanding a change in the system that made them pay enormous taxes while the nobles paid almost nothing. They criticized the king's beautiful wife, Marie Antoinette, whom they accused of spending vast sums of money. The people believed the only answer was violent rebellion, and the French Revolution began in 1789. Louis and his family were forced to leave Versailles and live in Paris. In 1792, Louis and Marie Antoinette were condemned for treason by the people, and executed—Louis in Jan-

uary 1793 and Marie in October.

Louis XVII (1785–1795) was the son of Louis XVI. After his father was executed in 1793, Louis was named king of France by the supporters of the monarchy. But the young prince was imprisoned by the leaders of the French Revolution and was never crowned. He died in prison at the age of ten.

Louis XVIII (1755–1824) was declared king of France by his supporters after the death of his nephew, Louis XVII. As a prince, he had escaped from France before his brother, Louis XVI, was executed. After Napoleon was defeated in 1814, the elderly king returned to Paris. He ruled there for the next ten years except for a time in 1815, when Napoleon returned to France and regained control for a few months.

ALSO READ: CHARLEMAGNE, CRUSADES, ENGLISH HISTORY, FEUDALISM, FRENCH HISTORY, FRENCH REVOLUTION, HUNDRED YEARS' WAR, ITALIAN HISTORY, VERSAILLES, VIKINGS.

▲ *Louis XVIII, seen here with members of his family, was king of France in name from 1795 and in fact from 1814, after Napoleon had been overthrown.*

No European king lived in more splendor than Louis XIV. He wore elaborate wigs and shoes with diamond-studded heels. He hired an army of men to build, furnish, and lay out the gardens in his vast palace at Versailles. The gardens covered an area of 250 acres (100 hectares), and it is said that four million flower bulbs were brought from Holland each year to add color. There were fountains and waterfalls everywhere, all powered by a special pumping station. The palace housed over a thousand courtiers, with four times that many servants.

LOUISIANA The colorful traditions of the early French and Spanish settlers in Louisana are still a part of life in the state today. The descendants of these settlers are called *Creoles*. The Spanish style of decorating buildings with lacy ironwork can be seen in the old part of New Orleans. Some people in Louisiana still speak a

LOUISIANA

form of French, called Creole. Louisiana has a civil legal system that is based largely on the French Napoleonic Code.

The Land and Climate Louisiana is a gulf state. It is not only on the Gulf of Mexico, but it is partly in it. The coast is lined with islands and *peninsulas* (pieces of land nearly surrounded by water). The largest peninsula is formed by the Mississippi Delta. The great Mississippi River carries soil downstream and deposits it at the river's mouth. The soil deposits grow, forming a new land area. The delta grows more than a mile (1.6 km) every 17 years.

Most of the land in Louisiana is a low-lying plain. The highest point is Driskill Mountain, 535 feet (163 m) high. It is in the northern section of the state. From here the land slopes southward toward the gulf. The southern third of the state is only 50 feet (15 m) above sea level. The lowest point, which is in the city of New Orleans, is five feet (1.5 m) below sea level. Thick walls of earth and stone keep the lowlands from being flooded.

Louisiana has more than 7,000 miles (11,265 km) of waterways deep enough for boats. The Mississippi and Red rivers are the two main rivers. Many *bayous* are located in southern Louisiana. Bayous are slow-moving streams that flow through swamps. The French people who came from Acadia (now Nova Scotia) in Canada to settle in the bayou country in the 1700's are called *Cajuns*, which comes from the word "Acadian." The state also has many lakes.

Louisiana has a semitropical climate. Summers are hot and humid, and winters are short and mild. The state has plenty of rain throughout the year. Its climate is just right for numerous crops.

History Many different Indian tribes once lived in the area of present-day Louisiana. The Caddoan group lived in the northwestern corner of the state. The Tunicans lived in the eastern and southern part of Louisiana. The Muskogean group lived in the eastern and central areas.

The lower Mississippi area was visited by early Spanish explorers, including Cabeza de Vaca about 1528 and Hernando de Soto in 1541. A French expedition led by the Sieur de La Salle came down the Mississippi River in 1682. At the river's mouth, on April 9, La Salle claimed all the land in the Mississippi basin for France. His claim included the basins of the rivers that flowed into the great river, too. He named the vast territory Louisiana in honor of his king, Louis XIV.

The French used only a small portion of the land they claimed. They founded New Orleans in 1718. Its location on the Mississippi and near the Gulf of Mexico made it an important port for ocean and river trade. It guarded one of the main water routes into North America. France lost Louisiana at the end of the French and Indian War. The part east of the Mississippi went to Britain. The part west of it went to Spain.

By 1800, France had taken the Spanish part back again. The United States bought the area extending from the Mississippi River to the Rocky

▼ *Although New Orleans is famous for its long history and old French Quarter, it thrives today because of its business and industry.*

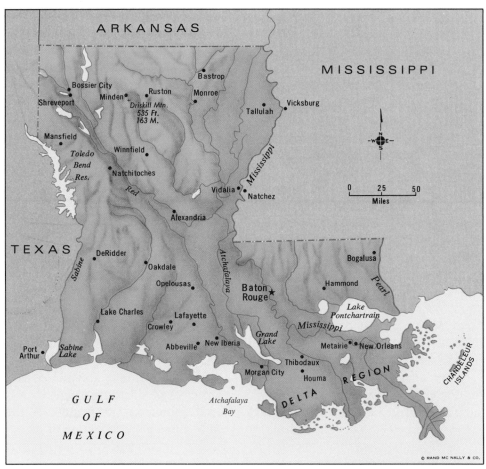

ARKANSAS

MISSISSIPPI

TEXAS

Bossier City
Shreveport
Minden
Ruston
Bastrop
Monroe
Vicksburg
Mansfield
Driskill Mtn.
535 Ft.
163 M.
Tallulah
Winnfield
Natchitoches
Vidalia
Natchez
Alexandria
Toledo
Bend
Res.
Red
Mississippi
Sabine
Atchafalaya
DeRidder
Oakdale
Opelousas
Bogalusa
Baton
Rouge
Hammond
Pearl
Lake
Charles
Lafayette
Crowley
Grand
Lake
Lake
Pontchartrain
Mississippi
Port
Arthur
Sabine
Lake
Abbeville
New Iberia
Metairie
New Orleans
CHANDELEUR
ISLANDS
Thibodaux
Morgan City
Houma
DELTA
REGION
GULF
OF
MEXICO
Atchafalaya
Bay

N
W   E
S

0   25   50
Miles

© RAND MC NALLY & CO.

© RAND MC NALLY & CO.

LOUISIANA

Capital
Baton Rouge (369,000 people)

Area
48,523 square miles (125,674 sq. km)
Rank: 31st

Population
4,408,000
Rank: 20th

Statehood
April 30, 1812
(18th state admitted)

Principal rivers
Mississippi River, Red River

Highest point
Driskill Mountain; 535 feet (163 m)

Largest city
New Orleans (559,000 people)

Motto
Union, justice and confidence

Song
"Give Me Louisiana"

Famous people
Louis Armstrong, Pierre Beauregard, Van Cliburn, Lillian Hellman, and Huey Long.

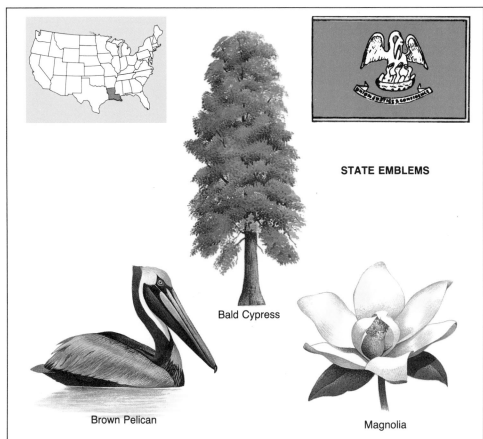

STATE EMBLEMS

Bald Cypress

Brown Pelican

Magnolia

▲ *New Orleans is well known for its annual Mardi Gras.*

Mountains from France in 1803. This land was called the Louisiana Purchase and included the area of present-day Louisiana. Louisiana, the first state to be carved from this huge piece of land, became the 18th state of the Union in 1812.

The War of 1812 put Louisiana in danger of attack. The British tried to capture New Orleans, but were defeated by General Andrew Jackson and his soldiers in the famous Battle of New Orleans in January 1815. This battle occurred two weeks after a peace treaty between the United States and Great Britain had been signed, but communication was so slow the soldiers had not received the news.

Two circumstances brought wealth to Louisiana in the years that followed. One was the river-and-ocean trade of New Orleans. The other was agriculture. Thousands of black slaves raised cotton and sugarcane on large plantations in the state. Louisiana voted to join the Confederacy and entered the Civil War in 1861. Union forces took over the state in 1862. The state was bankrupt after the war. Different groups began to struggle for power. On one side were the freed blacks and some whites. On the other were the whites who wanted to regain their power over the blacks. The tension lasted many years.

In the early 1930's, Huey Long became the most powerful politician in Louisiana. He served as governor of the state and as a senator in Washington. Long ruled like a dictator, but he made some social and economic reforms to help the people of Louisiana. He was assassinated at the state capitol in 1935.

Louisianians at Work History was made in Louisiana in 1901. Oil was discovered in that year. The discovery was made at just the right time—automobiles were soon to become popular. Today, Louisiana produces more oil than any state except Texas and Alaska. It leads the country in producing natural gas. (Like oil, natural gas comes from wells.) These two underground resources have given the state its biggest industry.

Manufacturing is second. Its two principal products are chemicals and food products. Oil refining is the third most important kind of manufacturing. Refineries produce gasoline and other products from oil.

Tourism is far below manufacturing in terms of the dollars it earns, but it is an important business in Louisiana. Visitors come from all over the United States to the annual Mardi Gras festival in New Orleans. The celebration includes colorful parades and gay costume balls. In French, Mardi Gras means "Fat Tuesday"—so called because it is followed by the very lean 40 days of Lent. The celebration is an old French custom and takes place on the Tuesday before Ash Wednesday—the day Lent begins.

Agriculture is also important. The principal crops, in order of value, are soybeans, sugarcane, rice, cotton, and yams (sweet potatoes). Livestock and animal products bring the state about one-third as much money as crops. Louisiana has a large fishing industry. A major part of the nation's shrimp catch comes from the gulf waters of Louisiana.

The old trapping trade of Indians

▼ New Orleans attracts tourists from all parts of the world. Among the city's many attractions is an active street theater.

and frontiersmen is still carried on in the woods and swamps of Louisiana. No other U.S. state earns as much money from the sale of fur as Louisiana. The woods also provide much timber.

ALSO READ: CIVIL WAR; CONFEDERATE STATES OF AMERICA; GULF OF MEXICO; HURRICANE; JAZZ; LA SALLE, SIEUR DE; MISSISSIPPI RIVER; RECONSTRUCTION; WAR OF 1812.

LOUISIANA PURCHASE The Louisiana Purchase has been called the most important event that occurred in our history during the first half of the 1800's. President Thomas Jefferson bought the entire Louisiana territory from the French in 1803. This territory extended from the Mississippi River to the Rocky Mountains and from the Gulf of Mexico to the Canadian border. It added almost a million square miles (2.6 million sq. km) of land to the south and west of the United States. The United States could then expand westward.

The Louisiana territory had been owned by European countries for many years. First France and then Spain controlled it. Napoleon, the French leader, regained Louisiana from Spain in 1800. The Spanish governor in New Orleans, however, did not know this, and closed the port to U.S. shipping. Americans needed the seaport to ship goods up and down the Mississippi River and to other countries. President Jefferson knew that France really controlled New Orleans. He sent James Monroe to Paris with an offer to buy the port from France for two million dollars.

Napoleon surprised Jefferson by offering to sell not only New Orleans but the whole Louisiana territory. Napoleon asked for 20 million dollars for all the land. But he later agreed to take about 15 million dollars. The United States paid France 11,250,000 dollars and agreed to pay French

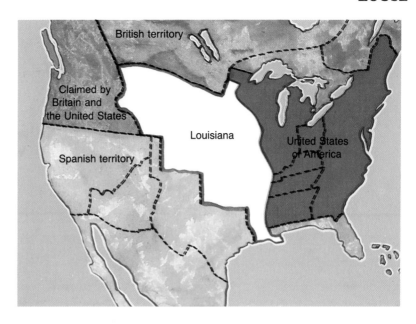

debts to U.S. citizens. The purchase treaty was signed on April 30, 1803. The territory made up all or part of what became 15 new states. The United States had bought enough land to double the country's size.

ALSO READ: JEFFERSON, THOMAS; LEWIS AND CLARK EXPEDITION; LOUISIANA; MONROE, JAMES.

▲ In 1803, President Thomas Jefferson bought nearly one million square miles (2,590,000 sq. km) of land from Napoleon. This transaction, the Louisiana Purchase, doubled the size of the United States.

LOUSE A louse is a tiny, wingless insect that can cause a lot of trouble. Lice are dangerous *parasites*—living things that live on or in other animals. These insects, which look like tiny crabs, cause great discomfort and spread serious diseases.

There are two main types of lice—biting lice and sucking lice. Biting lice have mouth parts that are made for chewing and biting. They usually live on birds, and eat flakes of dried skin and feathers. Sucking lice have mouth parts that are specifically made for piercing skin and sucking blood. They live on many mammals. Their bodies are flat, and they have powerful claws that grip an animal's hair and make them hard to pull off. Both biting and sucking lice cause much itching. Sucking lice also spread disease. They are the main carriers of typhus fever.

In 1528 the tiny louse decided the outcome of a war. Louse-borne typhus broke out among French troops besieging a Spanish army in Naples. In just 30 days half the French army had died from the disease, and the rest were defeated. Lice had made Spain's ruler the master of Europe.

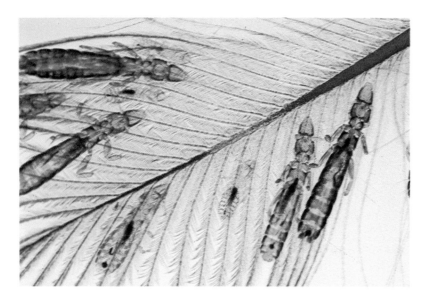

▲ *Lice clustering on a pigeon's feather. Bird lice have often evolved along with the birds on which they are parasites. Scientists are able to use this fact. By examining the lice on different types of birds, they can gain clues about whether the types of birds are related.*

▼ *The Louvre, the great art museum in Paris, was originally a palace of the French kings. The main parts were built in the reign of Louis XIV (1638–1715).*

Body and head lice can attack human beings. They live in people's hair, where they attach themselves to the strands. They lay their eggs, called *nits*, in the hair, or in the seams of clothing. Anyone with lice should get medical treatment.

ALSO READ: INSECT, INSECT PEST, PARASITE.

LOUVRE For hundreds of years, the Louvre was a great royal palace in the city of Paris. Various kings had added new buildings to the huge estate and had artists redecorate the older buildings. The leaders of the French Revolution decreed that all works of art seized from the royal palaces, the homes of nobles, and from the convents and churches should be brought to the Louvre.

The Louvre is now one of the world's largest art museums. It covers almost 50 acres (20 hectares) on the north bank of the Seine River. The museum's 140 exhibition rooms house about 275,000 works of art, including about 5,000 paintings. Among the Louvre's greatest treasures are the ancient Greek statues, *Venus de Milo* and *Victory of Samothrace*, and Leonardo da Vinci's painting, *Mona Lisa*. The only U.S. artists represented are Mary Cassatt and James Whistler. One of Cassatt's mother-and-child paintings hangs in the Louvre, and so does Whistler's famous painting of his mother.

All the works of art in the Louvre were removed and hidden in different places throughout France during World War II. After the war, they were all returned.

LOW COUNTRIES The term "Low Countries" is given to a flat region between France and Germany. It consists of Belgium, Luxembourg, and the Netherlands (Holland). The entire region was once called the Netherlands, a name meaning "low countries." Julius Caesar's Roman armies invaded the area in 58 B.C., but the Franks, a Germanic people, drove the Romans out in the A.D. 400's. The Low Countries became part of the Frankish kingdom, but in 870 they were split between the East and West Frankish kingdoms (now France and Germany).

The Low Countries were again united by the French dukes of Burgundy in the 1300's. In 1516, Charles, Duke of Burgundy, ruler of the Low Countries, became king of Spain. The region came under Spanish influence. The Roman Catholic Spaniards persecuted the Protestants in the Low Countries and, in 1581, what is now the Netherlands broke away. But Belgium stayed under Spanish rule until

1713, when Spain surrendered it to Austria.

From 1795 to 1813, France, under the leadership of Napoleon, ruled the Low Countries. In 1815, however, Belgium and the Netherlands united as the Kingdom of the Netherlands. Luxembourg was ruled by the king of the Netherlands, who was also the Grand Duke of Luxembourg. Belgium became a separate independent country in 1830. Luxembourg became largely self-governing in 1839, although the Dutch king continued to rule until 1890.

ALSO READ: BELGIUM, LUXEMBOURG, NETHERLANDS.

LOW, JULIETTE GORDON see YOUNG PEOPLE'S ASSOCIATIONS.

LSD see DRUG ABUSE.

LUBRICANT see FRICTION.

LUMBER AND LUMBERING
Look around you now and notice all the things that are made of wood. Even the paper of this book started out as wood.

Lumbering (the business of preparing timber for use in building and manufacturing) is one of the oldest and biggest industries in the United States. Lumber was important in the early development of the colonies, when settlers lived in log cabins, and had only wood for fuel. Many settlers were able to earn a living from logging, since lumber was needed both in the colonies and in Europe. At that time, most logging was done in New England. Today, most lumbering in the United States is done in the pine forests of the South and Pacific Northwest. The building (construction) industry uses more than half of the lumber, but the paper industry also uses much wood.

Russia and the United States are the world's leading producers of lumber. Canada, Brazil, Finland, Sweden, and China are also major lumber-producing countries.

Lumbering Logging is the first of the three main branches of the lumber industry. Foresters mark the trees that are to be *felled* (cut down). Then loggers fell the marked trees with power saws. The felled trees are cut into smaller sections, and these logs are taken to a sawmill.

Logs are sent through the sawmill on a moving belt. After the bark is removed from the logs, they are cut into boards. Then the lumber must be *seasoned*, or dried, since untreated wood contains a great deal of water. If lumber were not seasoned, it would stain, rot, and warp (twist out of shape) quite easily. Sometimes lumber is dried in the open air. But often it is dried artificially in a *dry kiln*. The boards are graded before and after they are seasoned according to their size, kind, and quality.

Lumber is finished, or given a smooth surface, at a *planing* mill. Lumber used in construction is also cut into the proper shapes for floors, shingles, and house trim.

Types of Lumber *Hardwood* lumber comes from deciduous trees (trees

▲ *A canal in the Low Countries winds lazily past a windmill.*

◄ *In lumbering, the top branches of a big tree are trimmed off before the tree is felled. This is done so the tree does not damage others near it as it falls.*

▲ *In Europe, the major wood-producing countries are Sweden, Norway, and Finland. Here, logs are being rafted down a Swedish river.*

▼ *Logs with their bark removed are piled outside a sawmill. They will be cut into lumber.*

that lose their leaves in autumn), such as maples and oaks. Hardwood is used primarily for floors, furniture, paneling, and tools. Conifers such as pines, firs, and spruce, produce *softwood* lumber. Softwood is used in construction and in making pulp, from which paper is made. (Pulp is wood that has been ground up and moistened.) The cellulose in pulp is used in making plastic, linoleum, and rayon. Plywood, used in construction, is made of several thin layers of wood glued together. Tar and turpentine are obtained from wood. Sawdust, from cutting lumber, is used as industrial fuel.

Conservation Loggers or lumberjacks consider the future of our forests when they fell trees. Lumber companies usually either reforest (plant new trees in) an area or leave some "seed" trees so that nature will reforest the region. In some areas, lumberjacks cut down all the old trees so that they will not die and create a fire hazard or fall on younger trees. Foresters also leave some trees on a hillside (called *selective cutting*) whose roots will grasp the earth and prevent soil erosion (removal of soil by wind and water).

■ **LEARN BY DOING**

Many wood products, such as paper and cardboard, can be recycled (ground up and reused) so that fewer trees need to be felled. Recycled wood is used to make such products as building boards, shoe boxes, paper towels, and newsprint. Find out if a group in your neighborhood collects paper and cardboard for recycling. If no one does, perhaps your class would like to start a recycling project. ■

ALSO READ: BARK, BUILDING MATERIAL, CONIFER, CONSERVATION, CONSTRUCTION, ECOLOGY, EROSION, FOREST FIRE, FORESTRY, FURNITURE, HOUSE, NATIONAL FOREST, NATURAL RESOURCES, SHELTER, TREE, WILDERNESS AREA, WOOD.

LUTHER, MARTIN (1483–1546) One of the greatest upheavals in the history of the Christian religion was started by a German monk named Martin Luther. Luther was born in Eisleben, Germany. He studied at the University of Erfurt, intending to become a lawyer, but he changed his mind and entered the Augustinian monastery in Erfurt. He became a priest in 1507. He was made a professor of religious studies at the University of Wittenberg, where he was very popular with his students.

Luther was not able to accept some of the practices of the Roman Catholic Church. In 1517, a Dominican monk named Johann Tetzel arrived in Wittenberg to sell *indulgences*; if people had committed a sin, they could buy an indulgence and be promised God's forgiveness. The money was to be used to help rebuild St. Peter's Church in Rome. On October 31, 1517, Luther nailed his Ninety-Five Theses (statements) to the door of All Saints' Church in Wittenberg. In them, Luther attacked the selling of indulgences. He said that persons received forgiveness by having faith in God and Christ and by showing they were sorry for having done wrong. He said that the Church was too interested in money.

This date in 1517 is considered the beginning of the *Protestant Reforma-*

tion. The Church under Pope Leo X tried many times to make Luther take back what he had said, but he refused. At a meeting in the city of Worms, Germany, in 1521, Luther said he could not go against his conscience: "I cannot do otherwise." He was excommunicated from (put out of) the Roman Catholic Church.

Under Luther's leadership, and with the support of the German princes, a large number of Christians split away from the Roman Catholic Church. Many other groups broke away from the Roman Church soon afterwards. Luther married Katharina von Bora, a former nun, in 1525, and they had six children. He translated the Bible from Latin into German and wrote many hymns, including "A Mighty Fortress Is My God." Luther's religious ideas became the faith called Lutheranism.

ALSO READ: PROTESTANT CHURCHES, PROTESTANT REFORMATION, ROMAN CATHOLIC CHURCH.

LUXEMBOURG Old castles and walled towns give Luxembourg a medieval look. It is a tiny picture-book country surrounded by France, Belgium, and West Germany. Rivers have carved deep valleys into the rocky hills. Along the rivers are peaceful and attractive little villages built during the Middle Ages. The nation's official name is the Grand Duchy of Luxembourg.

Most Luxembourgers are of French, German, or Belgian origin and belong to the Roman Catholic church. They speak French and German. Their own language is a mixture of these two, called Luxembourgish. The Luxembourgers mostly work in banking and industry, especially iron and steel. In the southwest, the country has some of Europe's richest iron mines.

The country's largest city, also called Luxembourg, is the capital. This lovely city has many bridges because two winding rivers, the Alzette and Pétrusse, flow through it. The city developed around a strongly fortified castle, which was built about 1,000 years ago.

Luxembourg became a constitutional monarchy in 1839 under King William of the Netherlands as Grand Duke. The country was later invaded and occupied by the Germans during both world wars. Part of the Battle of the Bulge was fought there during World War II. U.S. troops liberated Luxembourg in both wars. Today, the country is a member of the North Atlantic Treaty Organization, the Benelux economic union with Belgium and the Netherlands, and the Common Market. Luxembourg was one of the original members of the United Nations.

ALSO READ: EUROPE, EUROPEAN ECONOMIC COMMUNITY, LOW COUNTRIES, NORTH ATLANTIC TREATY ORGANIZATION, WORLD WAR I, WORLD WAR II.

▲ *Martin Luther, the "turbulent priest" whose public rejection of corrupt practices in the Roman Catholic Church of his time led to the Protestant Reformation.*

LUXEMBOURG

Capital City: Luxembourg (86,000 people).
Area: 998 square miles (2,586 sq. km).
Population: 370,000.
Government: Grand duchy.
Natural Resources: Iron ore.
Export Products: Iron and steel goods.
Unit of Money: Luxembourg franc.
Official Languages: French, Luxembourgish.

In Macao, tourists visit the Kwan Yin temple and its nearby garden. The first treaty between the United States and China was signed here on July 3, 1844.

MACAO Macao or Macau has been classed since 1974 as a Chinese territory ruled by Portugal. It is the oldest European settlement in the Far East. Cobblestone streets, brightly colored houses, and medieval Portuguese churches blend with Chinese shops and Buddhist temples. Chinese junks (boats) visit the harbor.

Macao is situated on the southern coast of mainland China at the mouth of the Canton River. Part of the territory lies on a peninsula. The islands of Taipa and Colôane to the south are also part of the territory. The total area covered is only six square miles (16 sq. km). The monsoons bring warm, wet summers and cool, sunny winters.

Hong Kong lies 40 miles (64 km) east across the Canton River delta. Ferries travel to Macao from Hong Kong and from Canton, China, about 70 miles (113 km) north of Macao.

About 99 percent of the people in Macao are Chinese. The others are Portuguese or mixed Portuguese and Chinese. The main religion is Buddhism. There are about 17,000 Roman Catholics. The official language is Portuguese, but Chinese, mainly Cantonese, is spoken.

Fishing is an important industry in Macao and provides the chief local food supply. Most of Macao's food and all of its fresh water are imported from mainland China. Macao has recently thrived as a gambling haven and as a port of entry for trade to China. Fireworks, textiles, and toys

▼ *A busy street in Macao, a Portuguese province and port in southern China.*

are manufactured in Macao.

In 1557, China agreed to let the Portuguese settle and establish a trading post in Macao. For almost 300 years, the Portuguese paid China for use of the land. In 1849, Portugal declared Macao a *free port* (port with no import duties on certain foreign goods). Portugal's right to the territory was recognized by China in 1887. It was an overseas province of Portugal from 1961 to 1974. In 1986, Portugal and China held talks to discuss the future of Macao and its eventual return to China.

ALSO READ: CHINA, PORTUGAL.

MacARTHUR, DOUGLAS (1880–1964)

"I shall return," U.S. General Douglas MacArthur promised the people in the Philippines when Japanese troops forced him to leave the islands in February 1942. He kept his promise, and his forces drove the Japanese out of the Philippines in 1945. MacArthur accepted the Japanese surrender in World War II aboard the U.S.S. *Missouri* in Tokyo Bay on September 3, 1945.

MacArthur was born on an army reservation in Little Rock, Arkansas. His father, Arthur MacArthur, was a Union colonel in the Civil War and a U.S. general in the Spanish-American War. Douglas graduated from the U.S. Military Academy at West Point in 1903, at the head of his class. He served as a colonel and later as a brigadier general in Europe during World War I. He returned to the United States after the war and became superintendent of the U.S. Military Academy. He was appointed chief of staff in 1930, becoming, at 50, the youngest man to hold this position.

President Franklin Roosevelt appointed MacArthur commander in chief of U.S. armed forces in the Far East when the United States entered World War II, in December 1941. MacArthur was chosen supreme com-

mander of all Allied forces in the Southwest Pacific in 1942 and led the Allied troops to victory. He was put in charge of setting up a democratic government in Japan after the war. He became commander of the United Nations forces in Korea when the Korean War broke out in June 1950. He thought he could end this conflict by attacking military bases in Red China, but President Harry Truman disagreed with him and dismissed him in April 1951. MacArthur was honored by the U.S. Congress in 1962 for his great leadership.

▲ *General Douglas MacArthur, U.S. military leader in the Pacific.*

ALSO READ: ARMY, KOREAN WAR, PHILIPPINES, WORLD WAR II.

MACDONALD, JOHN A. (1815–1891)

Sir John Alexander Macdonald was a great statesman and the first prime minister of Canada. He was born in Glasgow, Scotland, in 1815. When he was a young boy, his family moved to Canada, and he was brought up in Ontario. Macdonald's parents were able to send him to school only until he was 15 years old. After that, they arranged for him to become a lawyer's assistant. Macdonald soon became a lawyer himself, and a highly respected leader in the town of Kingston.

Macdonald opposed the old-fashioned, conservative views of the political leaders in Canada. He played a leading role in making the Conservative Party more modern and up-to-date. Macdonald was one of the first to work for a united Canada that would include the seven remaining British colonies in North America and stretch from coast to coast. With the help of a newspaper publisher named George Brown, Macdonald was successful in bringing about the creation of Canada in 1867. He became the country's first prime minister that same year. In all, he was prime minister four times, the last time being in 1878–1891.

▲ *John A. Macdonald, first prime minister of the Dominion of Canada.*

Macdonald's government purchased the Northwest Territories from the Hudson's Bay Company and began construction of the Canadian Pacific Railway.

ALSO READ: CANADA, FATHERS OF CONFEDERATION.

MACEDONIA The region of southeastern Europe known as Macedonia has a very ancient history. Macedonia is in the Balkan Peninsula on the northern coast of the Aegean Sea.

The region was settled around 3000 B.C. by wandering tribes. Tribes from the neighboring countries of Thrace and Illyria occupied parts of Macedonia around 2000 B.C. After 1000 B.C., the great civilization of ancient Greece was established to the south of Macedonia. The Macedonians admired the Greeks and copied many of their ways.

In 359 B.C., King Philip II became ruler of Macedonia and began a campaign to extend the borders of his country. He invaded Greece and gained control over most of the Greek city-states. Philip was assassinated, and his son, Alexander III (Alexander the Great), became king. Alexander, a brilliant military leader, built one of the greatest empires the world has ever known. He united all of Greece,

conquered Persia and Egypt, and even went as far as India. After Alexander's death in 323 B.C., the mighty Macedonian Empire fell apart. The Romans conquered much of it, and in 148 B.C. made Macedonia a Roman province. The Roman Empire split in two in A.D. 395, and Macedonia became part of the Byzantine, or Eastern Roman, Empire. Many other conquerors—Bulgarians, Turks, and Serbians—have since invaded the mountainous land of Macedonia.

Today, Macedonia is divided into three parts, belonging to Bulgaria, Yugoslavia, and Greece. Thessaloniki, in the Greek part, is Macedonia's largest city. Farming and mining are the most important occupations in Macedonia. Grain, tobacco, and fruit are grown; sheep and goats are raised; iron, copper, and other minerals are mined. The people are descended from many different nationalities. The southern Macedonians mainly speak Greek. The northerners speak Bulgarian or Macedonian.

ALSO READ: ALEXANDER THE GREAT; BULGARIA; GREECE; GREECE, ANCIENT; YUGOSLAVIA.

MACHIAVELLI, NICCOLÒ (1469–1527) Many modern-day ideas about politics and government were first written about in the 1400's and 1500's by Niccolò Machiavelli, an Italian statesman and soldier.

Machiavelli was born in Florence, at a time when Italy was completely divided into independent city-states. In 1494, when Machiavelli was a young man, the powerful Medici family, which had ruled Florence for many years, was overthrown. He was given an important position in the new government.

It was the general custom of the time to hire soldiers. Machiavelli started a "citizen's army" in Florence, believing that the natives of

▼ *The tomb of King Philip II of Macedonia. The massive gold coffin was discovered in 1977 in northern Greece, in the area where archeologists had long believed the ancient Macedonian capital of Aeges had been located.*

Florence would be more patriotic and better defenders of the city than hired soldiers. Machiavelli's duties required him to make many trips to the various governments of Italy, France, and Germany. In those countries, he was able to see how the rulers schemed to stay in power.

Machiavelli was banished from Florence when the Medicis came to power again. During his exile, he wrote *The Prince*, stating his ideas about how a country should be governed. Machiavelli wanted Italy to be united into one nation. He believed that this could only be achieved by one strong leader who had unlimited powers and was not bound by tradition. He dedicated *The Prince* to Cesare Borgia, an Italian soldier-statesman who wanted to rule all of Italy and often used treachery to get what he wanted.

The word "machiavellian" is used today to describe someone or something that is shrewd and cunning.

ALSO READ: FLORENCE, ITALIAN HISTORY, MEDICI FAMILY.

MACHINE A machine makes our work easier, because the machine itself does some of the work. A machine does work by changing the size or direction of a force. All machines are made up of one or more of the three basic (simple) machines—inclined plane, lever, and wheel and axle. There are three other "simple" machines—pulley, wedge, and screw—that are variations of the first three. (Often we call an electrical or electronic device—e.g., a computer—a machine, but here we are talking about mechanical devices.)

The *inclined plane* is the simplest machine. It makes lifting easier. The object must be moved a greater distance, but less force is needed to move it. When you walk up a ramp for example, you are using an inclined plane to lift your body.

If you have ever pried a rock up with a stick, or punched a hole in a can with a can opener, you have used a *lever*. A lever is just a rigid body, such as a stick or a crowbar, that pivots (turns) around a fixed point. The fixed point is at the *fulcrum*. The force can be applied at any point on the lever, and the weight to be moved, or the resistance to be overcome, can be at any other point.

Let's say you want to move a large rock, and you have a strong stick to use as a lever and a block of wood to use as a fulcrum. You place the block of wood close to the front of the rock and lay the stick across the block. Push the far end of the stick under the rock and press down at the near end.

By pushing down with a fairly light force, you can lift the rock, which has a heavy downward force or weight. But you have to push a fairly long distance, and the rock only moves a small distance.

The lever has changed the size of the force—you push down with a small force at one end of the lever, and at the other end this force is large enough to move the rock. The lever has also changed the distance through which the force moves—you have to push a long distance, but the force at the other end of the lever only moves the rock a small distance. The lever has also changed the direction of the force—you push down and the rock moves up.

With a *wheel and axle*, the force is usually applied at the center of the wheel—the axle. The wheel acts like a continuous lever, carrying the force from the axle to the rim. At the rim, the force is less, but it is moved through a greater distance. When you pedal a bicycle, you push down hard but only for a short distance. The force that finally reaches the rim of the wheel is smaller, but it moves you farther, because the bicycle wheel is a bigger circle than the circle through which the pedals are turning.

A wheel and axle can also work in

▲ *Niccolò Machiavelli, Italian political philosopher.*

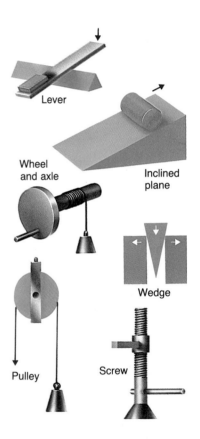

▲ *Simple machines. Machines change one type of work into another, most often to make it easier to do something. Usually, this means you do a little work over a long distance so that the machine can do a lot of work over a short distance. For example, in the screw set-up shown here (jackscrew), you have to turn the lower bar many times to raise the upper bar only a little, but this bar can raise a very great weight.*

▲ *Alexander Mackenzie reaches the Pacific Ocean after his long journey across the northern part of North America.*

▲ *An aerial view of the Mackenzie River delta in Canada's Northwest Territories.*

the opposite way—a small force applied to the rim is turned into a large force at the axle. Or both forces can be operative at the rim, so that only the direction of force is changed—as in rolling a barrel.

A *pulley* and a wheel work like a circle of levers. A simple pulley is just a rope thrown over a wheel. You pull the rope down on one side of the pulley to lift a weight on the other side. The simple pulley changes the direction of force. Using a combination of several pulleys, you can lift heavier weights with less effort.

A *wedge* is a double inclined plane. A small force hitting the back of the wedge becomes a larger force at the sides of the wedge. But the force at the sides doesn't move so far as the force at the back.

A *screw* is an inclined plane that curves around a center. A wood screw changes the turning force of the screwdriver into a straight-ahead force that bites into the wood.

You probably use all of these simple machines every day. In opening a bottle or writing with a pencil, you use simple machines.

ALSO READ: ENERGY, ENGINE, FRICTION, GEAR, MOTOR, PERPETUAL MOTION, PHYSICS.

MACKENZIE, SIR ALEXANDER
(about 1760–1820) Sir Alexander Mackenzie was the first white explorer to cross the continent of North America to the Pacific Ocean. He traveled through the wild regions of northwest Canada.

Mackenzie was born in Stornoway on the island of Lewis, off Scotland. He moved to New York as a child. A few years later, he went to Montreal, Canada, and joined the fur-trading North West Company in 1778. He was stationed at a trading post on Lake Athabasca in northern Alberta. His outpost, Fort Chippewyan, was at the edge of the wilderness. No

Europeans knew what lay beyond to the north or west. Mackenzie was determined to find out. In 1789, he traveled north on the huge river that was later named after him, to where it reaches the Arctic Ocean. Mackenzie was a strong man and a tireless paddler. He led his exploring party in three large canoes more than 1,000 miles (1,600 km) to the Arctic Ocean, traveling at the almost unbelievable average rate of 99 miles (160 km) a day.

Mackenzie returned to Fort Chippewyan, but in May 1793 he set out to the west. His route lay through the Rocky Mountains. He followed dangerous, twisting rivers never before explored, narrowly missing death many times. He reached the Pacific coast of what is now British Columbia after two months. Mackenzie then traveled back to eastern Canada. He later returned to Britain, where he was knighted. He died in Scotland.

ALSO READ: CANADA, FUR, MACKENZIE RIVER.

MACKENZIE RIVER
Take a look at the map of Canada. Put your finger on Great Slave Lake in Canada's Northwest Territories. Now trace the path of the Mackenzie River as it flows out of Great Slave Lake northwestward to the Arctic Ocean. Another large river—the Slave River—flows into Great Slave Lake from the south. Before it reaches Great Slave Lake, it is joined by the Peace River, which starts high in the Rocky Mountains. If you paddled a canoe from the beginning of the Peace River, across Great Slave Lake, and then down the length of the Mackenzie River, you would have traveled about 2,635 miles (4,240 km)!

The Mackenzie-Peace River System is the second longest waterway in North America. (The Mississippi-Missouri River System is the longest.)

Small ships can travel about 1,700 miles (2,750 km) along the Mackenzie-Peace System.

The Mackenzie River was discovered by the Canadian explorer, Sir Alexander Mackenzie, in 1789. He traveled down it hoping to reach the Pacific Ocean. He arrived at the Arctic Ocean instead, and named this river the "River of Disappointment." The name was later changed in honor of this brave explorer.

ALSO READ: CANADA; MACKENZIE, ALEXANDER.

MADAGASCAR Madagascar is the fourth largest island in the world. It is in the Indian Ocean, about 250 miles (402 km) off the southeast coast of Africa. The island is about 1,000 miles (1,609 km) long and 375 miles (603 km) wide at its broadest point—a little smaller than the states of Arizona and New Mexico combined. The country of Madagascar includes several small nearby islands.

This island country is rugged, with high plateaus and mountains. Mount Maramokotro in the north is the highest peak, at 9,462 feet (2,884 m). There are many extinct volcanoes in the Ankaratra Mountains near the center of Madagascar. Low plains lie between the mountains and the sea. The climate in the highlands is cool and pleasant and, in the coastal regions, hot and damp.

On a plateau surrounded by hills overlooking the east coast, the capital and largest city, Antananarivo, reveals both ancient and modern sides of the country. Modern buildings show French influence.

Plant and animal life on Madagascar are different from those found on the African mainland and in other countries. Among the rare animals are many types of lemurs (small, monkeylike animals). Fossil bones of strange prehistoric animals have been found there which have not been discovered elsewhere.

Although Madagascar lies off the coast of Africa, the country has an Asian appearance because of its people and their customs. The people are mostly either of African or Indonesian descent. They speak French and their own language, Malagasy. Farming is the most important occupation in Madagascar. Coffee is the chief export crop, and more than half of the world's supply of vanilla is grown on the coastal plains of Madagascar. Rice is the basic food, and its production is essential to the country's economy. Cattle are the most important livestock. Rich deposits of graphite, chromium ore, and other minerals are mined. Trade with other countries, such as France, is important.

Several thousand years ago, people crossed the Indian Ocean from the region that is now Indonesia and settled on Madagascar. Later, Arabs and other people from Africa came to the

▲ *More than three-fourths of the people of Madagascar live off the land.*

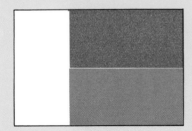

MADAGASCAR

Capital City: Antananarivo (700,000 people).

Area: 226,658 square miles (587,041 sq. km).

Population: 11,100,000.

Government: Republic.

Natural Resources: Bauxite, chromite, graphite, semiprecious stones.

Export Products: Coffee, vanilla, sugar, cloves.

Unit of Money: Malagasy franc.

Official Language: Malagasy.

The largest bird we know of was the extinct elephant bird of Madagascar. This flightless bird was up to 10 feet (3 m) in height and weighed about 950 pounds (430 kg). One of this giant bird's eggs is preserved in the British Museum (Natural History). It measures 34 inches (86 cm) around its long axis and 28 inches (70 cm) around its middle. The huge shell, seven times as big as an ostrich egg, would hold 2 gallons (8.8 liters).

island. Diego Dias discovered Madagascar for Portugal in 1500. Traders from other European countries followed him. In the late 1800's, the French seized the island and set up the colony of Madagascar. In 1958, the colony was given self-rule as the Malagasy Republic. France granted it complete independence in 1960. The Malagasy Republic was renamed the Democratic Republic of Madagascar in 1975, when the fourth in a series of military leaders took over the government. The country has since followed a socialist course, with many businesses controlled by the government.

ALSO READ: AFRICA, LEMUR.

▲ Dolley Madison, the wife of President James Madison, was a popular First Lady.

MADISON, JAMES (1751–1836)

"The great little Madison," as James Madison was called, was a small, frail man with a brilliant mind. He began his political career early, and helped draw up the U.S. Constitution more than 20 years before he became the fourth President of the United States. He was responsible for some of the basic ideas used in the Constitution. For that reason, he is gratefully remembered as the "Father of the Constitution."

James Madison grew up at Montpelier, a handsome plantation house that his father had built in Orange County, Virginia. He suffered from poor health, but studied hard, and enrolled at the College of New Jersey (now Princeton University) at the age of 18. He became interested in problems of government, and he was elected a delegate to the Virginia Convention in 1776. This convention declared Virginia to be independent of Great Britain several weeks before the Declaration of Independence was adopted. Young Madison was appointed to the committee that wrote the new state constitution. Later, he was a delegate to the Continental Congress (1780–1783).

Madison was chosen as delegate from Virginia to the Constitutional Convention of 1787. His "Virginia Plan" of government became a kind of basis for the Constitution which was written at this convention. He also helped to write *The Federalist Papers* with two other members of the convention, John Jay and Alexander Hamilton. This series of essays explained the new plan of government to the people. A new Congress took the place of the old Continental Congress after the Constitution became the law of the land. In 1789, James Madison was elected to the House of Representatives, and one of his first acts was to urge that some amendments be added to the Constitution. The first ten amendments that were adopted and *ratified* (approved) by the

---

JAMES MADISON

FOURTH PRESIDENT   MARCH 4, 1809–MARCH 4, 1817

Born: March 16, 1751, Port Conway, Virginia
Parents: James and Eleanor (Nellie) Conway Madison
Education: College of New Jersey (now Princeton University), Princeton, New Jersey
Religion: Episcopalian
Occupation: Lawyer
Political Party: Democratic-Republican
State Represented: Virginia
Married: 1794 to Dolley Payne Todd (1768–1849)
Children: 1 stepson
Died: June 28, 1836, Montpelier, Virginia
Buried: Montpelier, Virginia

states were called the Bill of Rights. This bill guarantees the basic rights, such as freedom of speech and of religion, of all U.S. citizens.

Madison served as Secretary of State under President Thomas Jefferson. During this time, U.S. seamen and ships were being taken over by both the British and French, who were at war. In 1809, Madison succeeded Jefferson as President. He tried to make the French and British respect U.S. shipping without going to war, but was unsuccessful. The War of 1812 broke out between the United States and Great Britain over this issue.

Madison was reelected President. The British invaded the country, and were approaching Washington in August 1814. The President left the capital hurriedly to hold a council with one of his generals. His wife, Dolley, was left alone with the servants in the Executive Mansion (now the White House). She had Gilbert Stuart's portrait of George Washington cut from its frame, and she gave it to two gentlemen from New York, who promised to take it to a safe place. Her quick action saved this famous portrait, which now hangs again in the White House, from destruction. Dolley then packed some of the President's important papers in a trunk, and took them away with her in a carriage sent by friends.

On August 24, 1814, British troops entered the city and set fire to the Capitol, the White House, and other public buildings. Then they retreated, fearing that U.S. troops were coming. The Executive Mansion was still standing when the Madisons returned, but it was blackened by fire. The inside of the building had been almost totally destroyed. The President and First Lady lived in several different houses until the Madison administration left office.

The war ended in December, 1814, and the country entered a period of nationalism later called the "era of good feelings." U.S. citizens wanted to build up their new country and stay out of foreign affairs. This era lasted far beyond Madison's administration, which ended in 1817. Madison spent his last years at Montpelier, Virginia.

ALSO READ: BILL OF RIGHTS; CONSTITUTION, UNITED STATES; CONTINENTAL CONGRESS; VIRGINIA; WAR OF 1812; WHITE HOUSE.

MAGAZINE One of the best ways of reaching a large number of people is to publish a magazine. Magazines are published and read in countries all over the world. They provide entertainment and information on a wide variety of subjects.

Unlike books, which are published only once, magazines are issued in periodic installments. Unlike newspapers, which are not bound together permanently, magazines are usually stapled or sewn together and have a cover. Readers often *subscribe* to their favorite magazines, which means that each issue is mailed directly to them as soon as it is published. Magazines are also sold at drugstores, markets, and newsstands.

One of the first publications that could be called a magazine was published in London in 1704. It was called the *Review*. Its publisher, and the author of most of its contents, was

The President's house was not always called the White House. James Madison had the mansion painted white after it was burned by the British in the War of 1812. People then began to call it the White House.

▼ *There are special magazines for boys and girls of various ages.*

a young man named Daniel Defoe, the man who wrote *Robinson Crusoe.*

In 1741, Benjamin Franklin published one of the first magazines in the United States. His publication, the *General Magazine and Historical Chronicle*, did not last very long, but many popular, successful magazines were started in the 1800's. The *Atlantic Monthly* was founded in Boston in 1857. It was first edited by James Russell Lowell, a famous U.S. poet. Because people then had few sources of entertainment and news, general magazines, such as the *Saturday Evening Post*, became widely read. In 1925, *The New Yorker* was begun and developed into one of the best literary publications.

In recent years, the market for many general-interest magazines has been reduced because many people obtain their news and entertainment from television. Today, many successful magazines serve special-interest groups.

Several new types of magazines have appeared in this century. A digest contains selected articles and stories from other publications, written in condensed (shortened) form. The *Reader's Digest* is the best known example. Weekly news magazines have also become popular. They contain news photographs, political cartoons, and articles on the week's news.

Magazines for Young People
Youth's Companion, begun in 1827, was the first U.S. magazine written especially for children. It soon became one of the most popular magazines in the country with both adults and children. It was followed in 1873 by *St. Nicholas*, edited by Mary Mapes Dodge, who also wrote *Hans Brinker, or the Silver Skates*. These magazines published children's stories written by many well-known writers. *St. Nicholas* also published stories and poems written by children. Robert Benchley, William Faulkner, and Edna St. Vincent Mil-

lay were successful authors who wrote for *St. Nicholas* while they were still children. *American Boy* and *Open Road* were popular with boys. The first comic books were made in the 1930's, and many are still popular with children today. Other children's magazines contain stories, interesting information, and ideas about hobbies and games. Your school library can give you a list of children's magazines. Most junior-high and high schools print their own magazines or newspapers containing short stories, poems, and articles written by students.

Publishing a Magazine The price of a magazine is often low. Therefore, magazine publishers do not make much money from sales to readers. Most magazines make a profit by selling advertising space. In fact, most magazines could not survive without advertising.

The editors of a magazine are the men and women who put together each issue. The editor in chief and his or her staff decide what kinds of articles an issue should contain. The editor in chief may then ask freelance (independent) writers for some or all of the articles. (These writers are often called contributing editors.) He or she may also assign articles to in-house (staff) editors and writers. In a large magazine, each editor is responsible for a different subject, such as politics, fashion, fiction, and art. After the articles are written, they must be checked by the editors. The editors must arrange with photographers for pictures to illustrate the articles. Many magazines use freelance photographers. Magazines with a large circulation (sell a lot of copies) have full-time photographers.

Each issue of the magazine, including the cover, illustrations, and the arrangement of articles, must be designed by the art director and his or her staff. The magazine is then printed, and copies are bought by read-

The weekly magazine with the largest circulation is the U.S. magazine *TV Guide*. In 1974 it became the first magazine to sell over a billion copies in one year.

ers either from newsstands, supermarkets, or through the mail.

ALSO READ: ADVERTISING, CARTOONING, CHILDREN'S LITERATURE, COMICS, COMMERCIAL ART, JOURNALISM, PRINTING, PUBLISHING.

MAGELLAN, FERDINAND

(about 1480–1521) The first expedition to sail all the way around the world was organized by the Portuguese navigator and explorer Ferdinand Magellan. Magellan died before the end of the journey. But his courage and leadership inspired his crew to complete the dangerous voyage through unknown seas.

Ferdinand Magellan was born in Sabrosa, Portugal. As a young man, he served with the Portuguese army in India. A sea route to that land, around the southern tip of Africa, had been discovered in 1497 by the Portuguese explorer, Vasco da Gama.

Magellan dreamed, however, of finding a shorter route to Asia by sailing around the Americas. He especially wanted to reach the Molucca (Spice) Islands, where cloves were grown. The Portuguese were not interested, but the Spanish king gave him five ships and about 240 sailors. In 1519, Magellan began his voyage across the Atlantic.

After sailing down the east coast of South America, Magellan discovered a narrow passage, or *strait*, running west. To the south was a wild and icy land. As the explorers sailed through the strait, they could see the fires in the Indian villages along the coast, and they named the land *Tierra del Fuego* ("land of fire"). The strait was later named after Magellan. In November 1520, the expedition sailed out into the Pacific Ocean. Magellan headed west, expecting to reach China in a few days. After several weeks, supplies ran out, and his crew began to die of starvation.

At last, after more than three months without sight of inhabited land, the exhausted and battered fleet reached what are now the Mariana Islands in the West Pacific. Refreshed and revived, those who had survived pressed on to the Philippines. There, a tragedy occurred. Magellan tried to make peace between two warring tribes and was killed.

Heartbroken, his crew returned to the two remaining ships. Under a new leader, Juan Sebastián del Cano, they set sail again. Magellan had planned for the expedition to go back to Spain by the way it had come. But the winds were too strong and one ship was wrecked. The last ship continued west, loaded with cloves and nutmeg from the Molucca Islands. In September 1522, del Cano and 17 survivors finally reached Spain, the first persons to sail around the world.

ALSO READ: EXPLORATION; GAMA, VASCO DA; NAVIGATION.

MAGIC

You may have been to a party where a clever entertainer called a magician, or conjurer, performs tricks. He or she may hold up an empty top hat, say the magic word—"abracadabra!"—and pull a rabbit out of the hat. The conjurer calls the trick magic, because few people watching can be certain how he or she makes the rabbit appear.

In ancient times, when events happened that people could not explain, they called them magic. When the sun suddenly disappeared in the middle of the day, this could only be magic. We now know that this is an eclipse. Such "magical happenings" were thought to be the work of the gods or spirits, who controlled all things. People called magicians (often called *medicine men* or *shamans*) were thought to be able to perform acts to make the gods and spirits do certain things. For example, if many months passed without rain, people asked a magician to perform special rites, or

▲ *Ferdinand Magellan, Portuguese navigator. He set off in 1519 with five ships to sail around the world. Only one ship returned. Magellan himself perished during the expedition.*

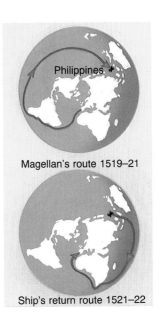

Philippines

Magellan's route 1519–21

Ship's return route 1521–22

▲ *A charm (amulet) from the Solomon Islands. It is believed to have magical properties to protect its owner against harm.*

▲ *The Indian Rope Trick, the most famous magic trick of all time, may be just a travelers' tale. "Karachi," shown here with his son "Khydar," claimed to have performed the trick in 1935, but his claim is not widely believed.*

▼ *The Magic Castle, a popular magic club in Hollywood. Here, magicians from all over the world meet to discuss their art and to present magic.*

ceremonies, to soothe the angry rain god. If the rain came, people thought the magician had brought it. Modern scientists have been able to explain most of the things that used to be called magic. But people in some parts of the world still believe in magic.

The actual methods magicians use to perform their tricks have varied widely at different times and in different regions. But most magicians use special words (charms such as "abracadabra"), songs, sayings, and gestures to cast their spells. They often have a collection of magical objects (such as herbs, bones, and pieces of someone's hair or clothing) that help them cast the spells. Some such objects and techniques are still considered magic by superstitious people. Have you ever heard that having a rabbit's foot is lucky? Have you ever seen people knock on wood when they say something hopeful? These superstitions are left from days when people thought magic warded off evil spirits.

Today, in the Western World, the word "magician" refers to an entertainer who performs tricks that seem to be impossible. He or she may make something disappear, find a coin behind someone's ear, "saw a person in half," or "read someone's mind."

Magicians' tricks are based on mechanical help or on their own skill at deceiving the audience. Magicians use *sleight of hand*, or *legerdemain*, to make small objects "disappear." Both of these terms mean quickness of hand. Magicians must be able to use their hands skillfully to get rid of the "disappearing" object before anyone notices. They must also be able to distract the audience's attention by talking or by using misleading facial expressions or gestures. A magician may juggle three balls and suddenly slip one of them up a sleeve while his or her eyes—and the audience's—follow the movement of the other balls.

The most famous U.S. magician was Harry Houdini (1874–1926). He specialized in escaping from many kinds of locks and chains. He would allow himself to be handcuffed and locked into a heavy metal container (perhaps filled with water), such as a trunk. He could get himself out of the trunk and the handcuffs within a few minutes. At one time, he had himself bound in ropes and locked in a packing case, which was then bound with steel tape. The case was then dropped into the New York City harbor, Houdini reappeared on the surface in 59 seconds.

■ LEARN BY DOING

Mind reading is an easy magic act to perform for a group of people. Arrange 12 different objects, such as playing cards, record album covers, or magazines, in rows on the floor. Say that, when someone picks one of these, you will read his or her mind to know which one he or she has chosen. Choose a friend to be your secret assistant. You and your assistant should decide on a secret code or signal to let you know which objects have been chosen. (The signal may be that your assistant will touch his or her left ear or clench a fist when someone points to the chosen object. Think of a signal that the others won't notice.) Then turn your back and close your eyes while a member of the group points to one of the objects.

When you turn around, someone in the group will point to one object after another. Your assistant, using the code, will let you know which was chosen. ∎

ALSO READ: ECLIPSE; FORTUNE-TELLING; HOUDINI, HARRY; WITCHCRAFT.

MAGNA CARTA The contract or agreement known as Magna Carta ("Great Charter") was one of the most important documents of all time. Magna Carta was an agreement between the nobles (barons) of England and the English king, John. It was signed in 1215. It reduced the power of the king and gave the barons certain rights and privileges. This was the first time in English history that such an agreement had been set down in writing.

Most of the later laws that helped England become a democracy were based on Magna Carta. In a democracy, the people or their elected representatives take part in the government of the country. In a democratic system, no ruler can gain absolute power. For example, Magna Carta stated that a council of barons and clergy should be set up. The king would have to get permission from this council before raising taxes or making any important decisions. This council became the basis of the present British Parliament, which is similar to the U.S. Congress. Magna Carta also stated that a person cannot be convicted of a crime except by the lawful judgment of his or her *peers* (equals). Trial by jury developed from this idea.

There were no written laws in England before Magna Carta. Instead, people were supposed to follow certain customs. For example, each noble or baron owed the king a certain amount of tax money. The king was not supposed to ask for a penny more. Such customs were part of a complicated organization of society known as the *feudal system*. When John became king of England in 1199, he needed extra tax money to fight a war with France. The barons did not want to pay higher taxes, but King John forced them to pay. The barons finally revolted. They wrote Magna Carta and had King John meet with them at a place called Runnymede. There, on June 15, 1215, the barons forced King John to sign Magna Carta. Magna Carta did not help all the English people. Only the nobles were considered important in those days. But in later years, the agreements of the charter were applied to everyone.

ALSO READ: DEMOCRACY; ENGLISH HISTORY; FEUDALISM; GOVERNMENT; JOHN, KING OF ENGLAND; LAW; MIDDLE AGES; PARLIAMENT.

MAGNET You may own a toy magnet, but magnets are more than toys. Large magnets are used to lift heavy pieces of iron and steel. Magnets are used in compasses. When you talk on the telephone, your voice travels through wires as electric signals. A magnet on the receiving end picks up these signals and makes them sound like your voice. Without magnets, we could not produce all the electricity we use in our homes.

More than 2,000 years ago, the ancient Greeks discovered *lodestones*, pieces of an iron ore named *magnetite* that are natural magnets. Lodestone can still be found today, but it is easier to make your own magnet.

■ **LEARN BY DOING**

You can make a magnet from another magnet with a large blunt needle (such as a tapestry needle) and a bar magnet (a magnet that looks like a stick). Slowly rub the needle with the magnet from the middle down to the point 25 or 30 times. You can rub with either end of the magnet, but do not change ends, and rub

▲ *The seal of King John on Magna Carta. This document, which John was forced to sign in 1215, greatly reduced the powers of English monarchs.*

▲ *The mineral called magnetite is a natural magnet. It is an ore of iron, and attracts iron objects.*

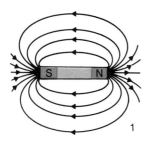

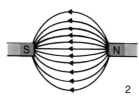

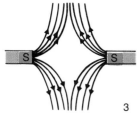

▲ *With two magnets, a sheet of paper, and some iron filings, you can show the shapes of magnetic force-fields. Put a magnet under the paper and sprinkle the filings on top (1). The filings show lines of force running between the north and south poles of the magnet. Now do the same using two magnets. You will see why a north pole attracts a south pole (2), and why two south poles, or two north poles, repel each other (3).*

in only one direction. Try to pick up a pin with the needle. If the needle-magnet does not work, rub it some more with the magnet. ■

How does a magnet work? Scientists believe that there are very small units, *magnetic dipoles*, present in all matter. In most substances the dipoles point every which way. But in substances like iron that can be magnetized there are *magnetic domains*—regions in which all the dipoles are pointing in the same direction—but the domains themselves do not all point in the same direction. However, when you magnetize this piece of iron, you pull all the domains in the same direction. The piece of iron has now only one, very large, domain. But, if you drop a magnet or hit it with a hammer, you shatter the one big domain into many small ones. All you have left is a piece of iron.

There are two types of magnets—*permanent magnets* and *electromagnets*. We have been discussing permanent magnets. Electromagnets need an electric current to work.

Permanent magnets are used for picking up small objects, holding refrigerator doors closed, holding objects such as ashtrays or pieces of paper onto metal surfaces, and so on. Electromagnets are now far more important than permanent magnets. Big ones are used in industry. Around the home, you can find electromagnets in doorbells, telephones, radios and TV sets, vacuum cleaners, tape recorders, furnaces, and other things run by electric motors.

ALSO READ: ATOM, COMPASS, EARTH, ELECTRICITY, ELECTROMAGNET.

MAGNIFYING GLASS see
LENS.

MAHLER, GUSTAV (1860–1911)
The composer Gustav Mahler was

born in a village in Bohemia (now Czechoslovakia). Ill-health constantly troubled the young Mahler, yet he threw himself into his great love—music—and also into physical exercise such as swimming and walking in the mountains.

He began composing at age 4, and at age 10 made his first public performance as a pianist. He studied at the Vienna Conservatory, and went on to become a professional orchestra conductor. At age 37 he was appointed director of the Vienna Court Opera.

Though he worked for many years in the world of opera, Mahler's own music was written in the form of symphonies and songs. He wrote his first symphony in 1888; like all his music, it expressed deep personal feelings. Some of his works call for large numbers of musicians; the *Symphony No. 8* (known as the "Symphony of a Thousand") requires eight solo singers, two choirs, and a full orchestra.

Mahler drove himself, and others, hard when working. He made enemies, and in 1907 he was asked to resign from the Vienna Court Opera. He also was told by doctors that he had incurable heart disease. He went to the United States, where he conducted the Philharmonic Society of New York, returning each summer to Europe to write music among the mountains he loved.

Mahler died in 1911, most of his music ignored. But today, his works are played and admired all over the world.

ALSO READ: COMPOSER, MUSIC.

MAINE
Maine lies the farthest north of any state in the eastern United States. It makes up the northern half of New England. It has almost as much land as the other five New England states put together.

Canada curves around northern

and eastern Maine. New Hampshire lies to the west of Maine and the Atlantic Ocean is south of Maine. The southern part of Maine is flat land. Toward the north and west, the land changes, becoming first hilly and then mountainous. The mountains are part of the White Mountain group, extending westward into New Hampshire. Maine's highest point is Mount Katahdin, 5,268 feet (1,606 m) tall, in Baxter State Park. The far northern part of the state is a thickly wooded plateau.

Maine has an irregular and rocky coastline. Many of the bays make fine harbors. Portland, the largest city in the state, is located on Casco Bay. Islands are sprinkled along the Maine coast. The largest is Mount Desert Island.

When most people think of Maine and the water, they think of the sea-coast. But the state also has more than 5,000 rivers and streams and 2,500 ponds and lakes. The largest lake is Moosehead, about 60 miles (97 km) northwest of Bangor. Other large lakes include Grand, Chamberlain, Chesuncook, Flagstaff, Rangeley, Mooselookmeguntic, and Sebago. The state's rivers are not used much for transportation because they have too many waterfalls. But the falls are a major source of hydroelectric power for industry. The most important rivers are the Penobscot, Kennebec, Androscoggin, Saco, St. Croix, and St. John.

Winters are cold and summers are cool in Maine. During the winter, greater amounts of snow fall in the western part of the state than in the eastern, seacoast region. The climate makes the state a popular place for sports all year round. Camping, fishing, and sailing are popular in the summer, and skiing is a favorite winter pastime.

History The coast of Maine was probably visited by the Vikings around A.D. 1000. John Cabot, an

Italian navigator in the service of England, supposedly explored the coast in 1498. In 1524, Europeans arrived on *La Dauphine*, a ship belonging to the French navy. Its commander was the great Italian sea captain, Giovanni da Verrazano. With him was his brother, Girolamo, a skilled map-maker. *La Dauphine* sailed north along the coast of North America. In May, it dropped anchor in Casco Bay, off the coast of southern Maine. Here the explorers met the Abenaki Indians. This tribal group, which spoke an Algonkian language, included the Malecite, Penobscot, and Pennacook tribes. They were hunters and fishermen. Verrazano noted the region's many harbors and its striking scenery. He returned to France and gave a good report of the area.

In 1604, some French people tried to settle on a small island in the St. Croix River. A hard winter and sickness killed half of the settlers. The rest left. Three years later, an English group started a settlement on the banks of the Kennebec River. This settlement fared no better than that of the French. Finally, in 1622, the English established a permanent settlement in southern Maine at Monhegan. Colonies were soon set up at Saco and Gorgeana (now York), the first English city chartered in North America. By the early 1620's, the

▲ Lobster traps are piled on the shore at New Harbor, one of many charming fishing villages along the coast of Maine.

The south Maine resort of Camden is famous as the place where the doughnut hole was invented by Captain Hanson Gregory in 1847.

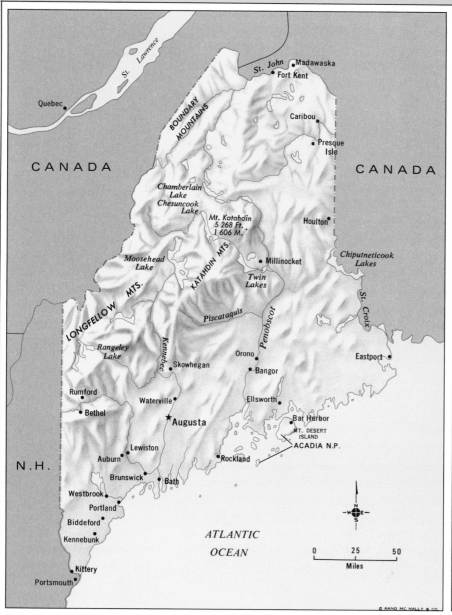

MAINE

Capital
Augusta (22,000 people)

Area
33,215 square miles (86,026 sq. km)
Rank: 39th

Population
1,205,000
Rank: 38th

Statehood
March 15, 1820
(23rd state admitted)

Principal river
Penobscot River

Highest point
Mount Katahdin; 5,268 feet (1,606 m)

Largest city
Portland (62,000 people)

Motto
Dirigo (I direct)

Song
"State of Maine Song"

Famous people
Hannibal Hamlin, Henry Wadsworth Longfellow, Sir Hiram Maxim, and Edna St. Vincent Millay.

© RAND MC NALLY & CO.

STATE EMBLEMS

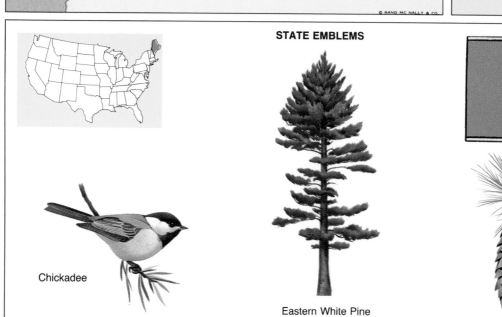

Chickadee

Eastern White Pine

White Pine Cone and Tassel

name Maine was being used.

Maine was made part of the colony of Massachusetts in 1647. It became a battleground during the French and Indian War and the Revolution. During the War of 1812, the British took the northern part of Maine. But they gave it back at the end of the fighting. A few years later, Maine was separated from Massachusetts. It became a state in 1820.

At Work in Maine The first English colonists in the region were fishermen and fur traders. Both fishing and trade turned them toward the ocean. The North Atlantic was dangerous for sailing vessels. It was especially hazardous during a northeaster—a fierce storm out of the northeast. In Maine fishermen's family records, the words "lost at sea" appear over and over beside the names of husbands and sons.

Before very long, the Indians, the fur animals, and the fur trade began to disappear. The Maine colonists then found that the beautiful pine forests around them could be cut down for lumber. They shipped some abroad and also used it to make ships.

Colonial fishermen and woodcutters were likely to be farmers, too. People raised crops during the summer. The rest of the year they did other work. A change came in the 1800's. The prairies south of the Great Lakes were opened to settlement. The rich soil there drew many New England farmers westward. But not all went. Maine has some of the level, fertile land that farmers like. Most of it is in big Aroostook County in the north.

Since the 1890's, the most valuable crop has been Aroostook potatoes. Only the states of Idaho and Washington produce more potatoes than Maine does. Apples are the state's most important fruit crop, followed by blueberries. Maine farmers also raise many broiler chickens, as well as turkeys, hogs, sheep, and cattle. Milk

and eggs are valuable dairy products.

There are industries in various parts of Maine. Lumbering is still important. This valuable natural resource is now chiefly used for making paper, toothpicks, boxes, furniture, and canoes. Maine is also a leading producer of leather goods, such as shoes.

Fishing remains an important economic activity. Lobsters, the most important single variety of seafood caught, account for half of the total annual income from fishing. Cod, salmon, bass, flounder, mackerel, herring, and haddock are also caught off the Maine coast.

Recreation and tourism are important businesses in Maine. Many visitors are attracted by the cool climate and beautiful scenery. Many people have built vacation homes on the seacoast or on lakes or rivers in Maine's pine country. Thousands of city dwellers from New York, New Jersey, and other mid-Atlantic states go north to enjoy a cool summer in Maine's climate. Tourists visit the state's parks, such as Acadia National park, with their scenic trails and campsites. Many also visit the Wadsworth-Longfellow House in Portland and the Old Gaol (jail) Museum in York. Other places of interest are Bar

▲ *Maine has many forests of spruce, poplar, birch, maple, oak and ash trees. Spectacular autumn colors attract many tourists to the state.*

▼ *The lakeside town of Sebago, Maine, with a background of beautiful fall colors. This popular tourist resort clearly illustrates the colonial character of much of New England.*

MAKEUP

Harbor on Mount Desert Island and Portland's famous old lighthouse.

ALSO READ: FRENCH AND INDIAN WAR; FUR TRADER; HYDROELECTRICITY; LONGFELLOW, HENRY WADSWORTH; VERRAZANO, GIOVANNI DA; WAR OF 1812.

MAKEUP Many people wear makeup, or cosmetics, on their faces in order to make themselves more attractive. Actors use makeup on their faces and any exposed parts of their bodies in order to change their appearance for the roles they are playing.

Stage makeup stresses highlights and shadows. In a theater, the audience is seated at a distance and cannot see the actors too clearly. The bright stage lights also make any normal coloring or ordinary makeup appear very pale, or washed-out. Dark makeup with heavy lines and shadows is needed simply to make the actors appear "natural."

Makeup used in television and motion pictures is lighter and less exaggerated, since the camera comes quite close to the face. But the bright lights still make the use of makeup necessary. For television, natural bone structure is emphasized. Colors to which the television camera is sensitive, such as green, blue, and violet, are used widely.

Besides the powder, rouge, mas-

▲ *People have been coloring their lips for thousands of years. Lipsticks are made from waxes mixed with dyes to produce the desired color.*

cara, lipstick, and other cosmetics in everyday use, theatrical makeup includes wigs, false beards, mustaches, and noses. *Putty* (a kind of wet clay) is used not only to create false noses, but also to make the bone structure of the entire face seem different. Beards and mustaches are stuck on the face with *spirit gum*. Makeup is used also on other parts of the body to create "wounds" or "scars" or just to cover blemishes.

Many different materials have been used as makeup throughout history. Since the late 1800's, the most popular theatrical makeup has been *grease paint*—a thick greasy solid that is made in the form of a stick.

An actor can look like almost anyone he chooses, with the careful application of makeup. If a young actor is playing the part of an old man, he can make his face appear older by drawing the lines and wrinkles of old age, adding putty to make his skin appear to sag, and wearing a white wig or beard. By using other makeup, an older actor can be made to look younger.

■ LEARN BY DOING

You might like to try using

▼ *Applying rouge to the cheeks is one of the oldest forms of makeup. Powder is made from minerals ground very fine and blended together.*

makeup to see what effects you can create. Ask an adult to let you experiment with some old cosmetics. Sit before a mirror in a well-lighted room. Try using light and dark bases to create shadows and hollows. Use an eyebrow pencil to draw lines extending from the corners of your eyes and mouth. Try to follow any natural "lines" or "creases" you already have. Be sure to wipe the makeup off carefully when you have finished "creating." Spread cold cream over the makeup and wipe it off with a tissue. Then scrub your face well with soap and water. Be sure to keep the makeup off your clothes. ■

ALSO READ: ACTORS AND ACTING, COSMETICS, DRAMA, LIGHTING, MASK, THEATER.

MALAGASY see MADAGASCAR.

MALAWI The Republic of Malawi is a narrow sliver of land that stretches about 500 miles (805 km) north and south along the western and southern shores of Lake Malawi in East Africa. The region was formerly known as Nyasaland. (See the map with the article on AFRICA.)

Malawi is slightly larger in size than Pennsylvania. It has very beautiful scenery, with high mountains, sparkling lakes, and fertile highlands. Sapitwa, the highest mountain in

Malawi, towers 9,843 feet (3,000 m) in height. The climate in the lowlands along Lake Malawi is hot and damp. But the highland areas are cool.

Most of Malawi's people, called Malawians, live in small villages and grow their own food. Tobacco, tea, and sugarcane are grown for export. Malawi has very few industries, and many of the people work in Zambia, Zimbabwe, and South Africa. Some factories in Malawi produce cement, bricks, textiles, shoes, and farm tools. A major road runs the length of the country. There are two railroads, one of which connects Malawi with the Mozambique ports of Nacala and Beira on the Indian Ocean. An international airport is located at Blantyre, the country's largest city. Lilongwe is the capital city.

The British explorer, David Liv-

▲ *Most of the people in Malawi live in villages in the country areas like this.*

Lakes take up almost a fourth of Malawi's total area.

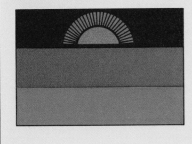

MALAWI

Capital City: Lilongwe (220,000 people).
Area: 45,747 square miles (118,484 sq. km).
Population: 8,000,000.
Government: One-party republic.
Natural Resources: Limestone, coal.
Export Products: Tobacco, tea, sugar.
Unit of Money: Kwacha.
Official Language: English, Chichewa.

The biggest bat is the Kalong fruit bat of Malaysia. One has been recorded with a wingspan of 67 inches (170 cm).

ingstone, was the first European to come to the region of Malawi, in 1859. He found the people almost destroyed by the terrible effects of the slave trade. In 1891, the United Kingdom took over the territory and set up the Protectorate of Nyasaland. In 1953, despite the objections of the Africans, it was joined with Rhodesia as the Federation of Rhodesia and Nyasaland. Independence was granted on July 6, 1964. The name was changed from Nyasaland to Malawi, the name of the people who once lived in the region. Malawi is governed by a president and a national assembly elected by the people.

ALSO READ: AFRICA, COMMONWEALTH OF NATIONS.

MALAYSIA Malaysia is a country of southeast Asia a little larger than New York State. The country is divided into two parts by the South China Sea. The mainland part is West Malaysia, on the Malay Peninsula. Thailand lies north of West Malaysia. The Malacca Straits border Malaysia on the west, and the South China Sea and islands of Indonesia are to the south and east. East Malaysia consists of the states of Sarawak and Sabah, which are 400 miles (645 km) away from the mainland on the island of Borneo. Kuala Lumpur is the capital of Malaysia. (See the map with the article on ASIA).

▲ *Tin being dredged from a wide and shallow river in Malaysia. Tin is Malaysia's most important mineral and a major export of the country.*

Malaysia is almost entirely mountainous, with narrow plains along the coasts, and a few fertile upland plateaus. Tropical rain forests cover most of the area—a wonderland of rare orchids, evergreens, bamboo, and palms. The climate in all parts of Malaysia is hot and wet, with an average rainfall of 100 inches (254 cm) in most places.

Many fields and hills in Malaysia are lined with rows of leafy rubber trees. Malaysia produces more rubber than any other country in the world. Thousands of people work on the rubber plantations. Other people are farmers who raise rice, tea, coconuts, fruits, and other crops. Additional rice must be imported to meet the country's needs. Many Malaysians

MALAYSIA

Capital City: Kuala Lumpur (1,000,000 people).
Area: 127,317 square miles (329,749 sq. km).
Population: 17,000,000.
Government: Constitutional monarchy.
Natural Resources: Copper, iron, lumber, oil, tin.
Export Products: Oil, palm oil, rubber, lumber, tin.
Unit of Money: Malaysian dollar.
Official Language: Malay.

work in the tin mines. Oil, tin, and copper are among the country's major natural resources.

The people of Malaysia are mostly of Malay, Chinese, and Indian descent. People from Sri Lanka and Pakistan also live there. The people of Malaysia show their different backgrounds through their languages, dress, religions, and festivals.

Traders from the Middle East, India, and Persia visited the area in the 1400's. The first European trading posts were set up in the 1500's. The region was controlled by the British for many years. In 1963, independence was declared and the new country was established as the Federation of Malaysia. It is now a member of the British Commonwealth. Malaysia is ruled by a sultan, who is head of state, and a prime minister, who heads the government. The parliament, or legislative assembly, is elected by the people.

ALSO READ: ASIA, BORNEO, RUBBER.

MALCOLM X (1925–1965)

Malcolm Little was born in Omaha, Nebraska, and grew up in Lansing, Michigan. His father, a Baptist minister, was a follower of Marcus Garvey, a black leader who urged U.S. blacks to return to Africa and establish a black nation. When Malcolm was six years old, his father was killed by unknown men who disagreed with his ideas about a separate black nation. Malcolm spent the next ten years in and out of foster homes and reform schools.

After completing the eighth grade, Malcolm moved to Boston to live with a married sister. His job as a railroad porter enabled him to travel to Harlem in New York City. Malcolm admired the "hip" people he met in Boston and Harlem. Soon he was involved in crime. He was sent to prison for robbery at the age of 20.

Malcolm read many books while in prison. He also heard about the *Black Muslims*, who followed a religion based on that of Islam and believed in a separate state for black people. Malcolm remembered Marcus Garvey. When he was paroled from prison, Malcolm became a spokesman for the Black Muslims. He changed his last name to "X" in the style of the Black Muslims.

In 1963, Malcolm X had a disagreement with Elijah Muhammad, the Black Muslim leader. He went on a pilgrimage (holy journey) to the Middle East. There he saw Muslims of all colors and nationalities worshiping together in true brotherhood. Malcolm realized that people could not be judged by the color of their skins. He returned to the United States to preach that, although black people should be proud of their African heritage, their future was in a really *United* States.

Many blacks (and whites) agreed. Some did not. Malcolm X set up the Organization of Afro–American Unity in 1964. On February 21, 1965, while speaking in Harlem, he was shot dead by an unknown person. Three days before his death, Malcolm X had spoken at Columbia University: "It is incorrect to classify the revolt of the Negro as simply a racial conflict of black against white. . . . We are interested in practicing brotherhood with anyone really interested in living according to it."

▲ *Rubber is Malaysia's most important export. It is obtained from large plantations of rubber trees. The country is still the world's leading producer of rubber, but today, synthetic rubber is taking more and more of the world market.*

Malcolm X began his self-education at the age of 20 while in prison. By reading and copying an entire dictionary he greatly improved not only his vocabulary but also his penmanship.

◀ *Malcolm X was once the spokesman of the Black Muslims. Later he preached harmony between people of all races.*

Malcolm X's followers said that his death was a sacrifice for the "black revolution."

ALSO READ: BLACK MUSLIMS, CIVIL RIGHTS MOVEMENT, ISLAM.

MALDIVES The Republic of Maldives lies about 350 miles (563 km) southwest of the tip of India in the Indian Ocean. It is a 500-mile (805 km) long chain of about 2,000 coral islands, called *atolls*, which are grouped together in 12 clusters.

The total area of the Maldive Islands is about one-fourth the area of the city of Los Angeles. None of the islands is more than five square miles (13 sq. km); most are much smaller. Also, none of the islands is more than 20 feet (6 m) above sea level. Malé, the largest and most populated island, is the capital. The islands have many lagoons and sandy beaches.

The climate of the Maldives is damp and hot, with heavy rainfall throughout the year. The humid weather produces a dense tropical growth of coconut palms, breadfruit, and fig trees on many of the islands. The Maldivians live on about 220 of the islands. Most of them make their living by fishing. Tuna and bonito fish are exported to India and Sri Lanka. Rice, one of the most important foods, must be imported.

Islam was brought to the Maldives in the 1100's and became the chief religion. For many years, Muslim sultans ruled the islands, which became a British protectorate in 1887. The British granted the Maldives complete independence in 1965. The Maldivians elect a legislature which appoints a president, who must then be confirmed by popular vote.

ALSO READ: ASIA, INDIAN OCEAN.

MALI The Republic of Mali is in northwest Africa. It is about three times the size of California and is completely surrounded by land. Mali links the countries of the Sahara Desert with the coastal nations of West

> The Maldive Islands abound in turtles with beautifully marked shells. The islanders fashion the shells into artistic objects.

▼ *A mosque at Mopti in Mali, built by slapping mud onto wooden scaffolding.*

MALDIVES

Capital City: Malé (46,000 people).
Area: 115 square miles (298 sq. km).
Population: 200,000.
Government: Republic.
Natural Resources: Fish.
Export Products: Fish.
Unit of Money: Rufiyaa.
Official Language: Divehi.

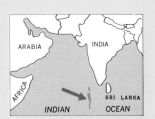

MALI

Capital: Bamako (800,000 people).
Area: 478,767 square miles (1,240,000 sq. km).
Population: 8,500,000.
Government: One-party republic.
Natural Resources: Iron, gold, phosphates, salt.
Export Products: Cotton, livestock, peanuts.
Unit of Money: Franc.
Official Language: French.

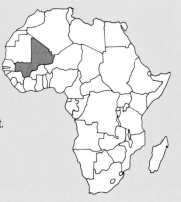

Africa. (See the map with the article on AFRICA.)

Two major rivers, the Niger and the Senegal, run through southern Mali. The capital city, Bamako, is on the banks of the Niger. The rainfall in this area is fairly heavy, and farmlands and pastures line the river valleys. In the extreme south of Mali is a flat region of grassy plains. Northern Mali is a hot area. It includes some of the southern fringes of the Sahara Desert.

The people of Mali are called Malians. Several different groups of people live in this large country. In the fertile river valleys, a people called the Bambara grow crops such as millet, rice, peanuts, and cotton. They also catch fish in the rivers. On the grasslands, the nomadic Fulani herd cattle, goats, and sheep. Another group of nomadic herders, the Tuareg, live in Mali's desert areas. Other peoples are the Malinke, Voltaic, and Songhai. Most of the factories in Mali are small food-processing plants. Exports are cotton, livestock, peanuts, and dried fish.

The region that is now Mali was once a part of several great West African trading empires. These empires—Ghana, Mali, and Songhai—flourished between the A.D. 300's and the 1500's. Timbuktu, one of the cities in Mali along the caravan trade route, became a center of learning for many Arab scholars during the 1500's. The University of Sankore was there. In the 1800's, the territory was occu-

pied by the French, who set up a colony called the Sudan. The Sudan united with the neighboring country of Senegal in 1959 to form the Federation of Mali. But the federation collapsed the following year. In September 1960, the Sudan declared itself the independent Republic of Mali. The army overthrew the government in 1968. The country has only one political party, but the president and parliament are both elected. Famine and drought have plagued Mali.

ALSO READ: AFRICA, SAHARA DESERT.

MALTA The five sunny Maltese Islands, lying in the Mediterranean Sea, form the independent nation of Malta. The nation's capital, Valletta, is located on the largest of the islands, Malta Island. The other islands are

During World War II Malta was heavily bombed by German airplanes. In 1942, King George VI of England awarded the George Cross (a medal for gallantry) to the entire nation of Malta, to honor the herosim of its people.

◄ *During World War II the Archbishop of New York visited Malta and witnessed the bomb damage of Senglea—then the most bombed city in the world.*

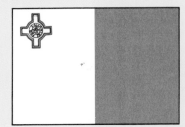

▲ Malta has several good natural harbors. This one is near the capital, Valletta.

peror Charles V granted the islands to the Catholic Order of St. John of Jerusalem (Knights of Malta). The Knights built the huge stone foundations and walls of the city of Valletta.

Malta was seized by Napoleon and his army in 1798. Two years later, the Maltese drove out the French, with the aid of the British. Malta became a colony of the British Empire in 1814, and became a vital British stronghold. But there were increasing demands by the Maltese people for greater freedom. Malta was granted home rule in 1961, and received its independence as part of the British Commonwealth in 1964. The country became a republic in 1974. It has an elected House of Representatives and the government is headed by a prime minister.

Gozo, Comino, and the tiny, uninhabited Cominotto and Filfla. Malta, Gozo, and Comino comprise only about 122 square miles (316 sq. km)—about twice the area of Washington, D.C.—but Malta is one of the world's most densely populated countries.

The strategic location of Malta—58 miles (93 km) from Sicily and 180 miles (290 km) from Africa—and its many excellent harbors have made it an important place for about 35 centuries. (See the map with the article on EUROPE.) Malta became a Phoenician colony around 1000 B.C., but earlier inhabitants of the islands had erected large, stone buildings and monuments that are still standing today. Malta was also ruled by the Carthaginians, Romans, Arabs, and Normans. In 1530, Holy Roman Em-

Many Maltese people work in the shipbuilding industry and at the former British naval dockyards. Others are farmers, raising wheat, potatoes, tomatoes, grapes, and citrus fruits in the tough, rocky soil. Most food, however, has to be imported. Fishing and wine-making are important.

In recent years, tourism has become one of Malta's largest industries. Visitors come from all over the world to enjoy the mild, sunny climate and beautiful beaches.

ALSO READ: MEDITERRANEAN SEA; NORTH ATLANTIC TREATY ORGANIZATION; PAUL, SAINT; PHOENICIA.

MALTA

Capital City: Valletta (14,000 people).
Area: 122 square miles (316 sq. km).
Population: 360,000.
Government: Republic.
Natural Resources: Limestone, salt.
Export Products: Clothing, textiles, ships, printed matter.
Unit of Money: Maltese lira.
Official Languages: Maltese, English.